With an eraser following me

Malin Bohman

WITH AN ERASER
FOLLOWING ME

Why don't I remember?
An autistic woman's musings
and searching for answers

Swedish original title:
Med ett suddgummi i bakhasorna –
Varför minns jag inte? En autistisk kvinnas funderingar och sökande efter svar
Copyright © Malin Bohman 2020, 2021

Translated by: Malin Bohman and Nouchine Hadjikhani
Copyright © Malin Bohman and Nouchine Hadjikhani 2021

Design of layout and cover: Malin Bohman
Figures: Malin Bohman
Cover images: javarman/Adobe Stock, freshidea/Adobe Stock
Fact-checking and good advice: Nouchine Hadjikhani

Publisher: BoD – Books on Demand, Stockholm, Sverige
Printed by: BoD – Books on Demand, Norderstedt, Tyskland

ISBN: 978-91-7969-008-3

In memory of my mother,
who, despite my memory problems,
will always be in my heart.

Content

Part I

Part II

Part III

Foreword

Memories of our own past are central to who we are, how we define ourselves, and how we take decisions and plan the future. Not being able to recall our own life events, whilst having an otherwise intact memory for facts, seems impossible to imagine. So when I first heard Malin describe to me what she was experiencing, I realized that it would be extremely difficult for me to put myself in her shoes, and try to understand how to see the world from her perspective. Hence I asked her to help me. I gave her an assignment: please write for me a few pages describing what it is like not to have an autobiographical memory.

I knew this was going to be fascinating to read, not only because it was such a puzzling topic, but also because I had had wonderful discussions with Malin, where she was sharing with me her thoughts, ideas, the books and articles she had read on or around the topic, and immediately I knew that she was what some call now an expert patient: an extremely well informed, intelligent person who would help me understand the way some people with her condition(s) experience life.

Being nursed during medical studies by Oliver Sacks' books, I had realized early the preciousness of listening to those who experience "strange" neurological symptomatology that alters their perception of the world. And now, Malin agreed to not only share this with me, but even go further and share with the world what it is to not only suffer from autobiographical memory difficulties but also to have an autism diagnosis – preceded by a series of inaccurate psychiatric diagnoses that had made – and in some instances continue to make – her life nightmarish at times.

Of course, the "few pages" I had asked for quickly started to become many more, and I am so excited to see that they eventually turned into a book! I am sure this must have been a very difficult exercise for her, but she never gave up, and was always in the quest of making her text better, more precise, expressing what she exactly meant, and I have to say how impressed I am by the results. Malin is indeed always seeking to make things right, and it became a subject of laughter between us when she would write to me that the final version was now written, only to a few days later let me know that she "only needed to make minor changes" here or there. She has been polishing this manuscript with utmost attention, and the results speak for themselves: here is a book that is both touching and full of valuable information, that reads like a novel at times, like a thriller at others, and like a textbook too.

So I have to say "Thank you, Malin!", for agreeing to work so hard to share your experience with the rest of us, and to make us aware of what it is to not only suffer through your many conditions but also to have been labelled a psychiatric patient, with all the difficulties that it can generate when trying to deal with physical ailments. I am sure that many will recognize themselves here and there, in their struggle with being autistic, with having memory difficulties, with being a patient in the system. And all readers will appreciate the very poignant content of this story of a journey through the meanders of an exceptional brain.

Nouchine Hadjikhani
Professor at Sahlgrenska Academy at Gothenburg University
Associate Professor at Harvard Medical School, Boston

Preface

*"Sometimes I have seen it all as being unreal, a dream to wake up from,
a nightmare that has a soul in my body.
Sometimes I have seen it all as a plague to endure.
When, in fact, it is just a different reality."*

Åsa Jinder

For many years, I have been thinking about why it seems almost impossible for me to get hold of memories of my own life – my autobiographical memories – and tried to find answers to this question. But unfortunately, I have not been able to find any solution among the caregivers I have had contact with over the years, nor in any of the many books I have read. At least no answers that have felt right within me, either emotionally or intellectually.

I have not either found any accurate descriptions of how it can feel and what it can be like to live with such difficulties, either in works of non-fiction or fiction. Or rather, I did come across some glances, sometimes – mainly in fiction books – but then, as I said, it has been just glimpses as well and nothing that described the situation in more detail.

I have been longing for answers as to why I have these difficulties. But even more so, I have been longing to find descriptions that I could really recognize myself in. Descriptions that might then have made me feel less alone and unsuccessful, as I have done over the years – and unfortunately still often do. And of course, I have also been longing to have my difficulties properly confirmed somewhere, to be believed and understood. At least to the extent that it is possible to understand such problems.

Therefore, it was quite remarkable that when I got in touch with Christopher Gillberg and Nouchine Hadjikhani, my story was then not only believed but also taken seriously. Later, they also gave me a more solid confirmation by showing that it was possible to see physiological abnormalities in my brain that could explain my memory difficulties. Thus, this helped me also to understand that this is not something I can modify, and it is not something I should either be ashamed of or feel so unsuccessful about.

After Nouchine showed me a study done in 2015, I have also understood that memory researchers have begun to take an interest in this memory problem after all. And I have also come across several people with similar difficulties online, so I now understand that I am not alone in having them. I should not say that the latter feels good, because this is not a difficulty I wish for someone else, but it still brings a sort of relief. The sad thing is that there is still so little information to be found about this kind of problem. Yes, it is almost non-existent.

So when Christopher and Nouchine suggested that they write a case report of me, I didn't say no but instead began to try to answer the questions Nouchine asked me. However, I had not expected my answer to be this long, even though I am not exactly known for my good capacity to be brief. And I really had no idea that it might even become a book. No, I probably would not have dared to start answering at all then.

***

I should probably also explain how I composed this text, how I was thinking when I wrote it. It can probably be best described by the fact that I usually think a lot. When I puzzle over a subject, a lot of ideas and questions usually come up. And over the years, this has also been the case in terms of wondering about my autobiographical memory. This is why I list in this book thoughts I have had over the years, lots of ideas, and even though many may be both a little wacky and inexperienced, I have not let myself been stopped by it but simply let my brain spin freely. And that despite the risk that it might then get a little crazy sometimes. You who possess excellent knowledge of our brain and its functions can thus feel warned. However, I can comfort you with the fact that in the last chapter, I will also give an account of at least some of what the researchers have found out. And in addition, you will in the appendix also find the case report I mentioned.

When I muse, I often do so in the form of a kind of conversation with myself, and this is how I have worked with this text. So sometimes, this becomes almost a discussion between two different Malin: one much younger and more sensitive version and one who is more distant and analytical. One who also possesses some knowledge in both psychology and neurology, but who over the years has come to the realisation that she should also take the time to have a dialogue with the younger version because they both have a lot to learn from each other.

Writing this has certainly been very useful to me. It has been a way for me to get all my thoughts gathered in one place, but also it has given me the opportunity to write about and process at least some of what I have experienced and gone through in psychiatry. Sadly, psychiatry mistreated me by misdiagnosing me, because the knowledge and understanding of many of my difficulties didn't exist then. But I will not deny that I also hope to be able to reach out to some of you who experience similar problems, especially if you, like me, feel very alone about having such difficulties and perhaps even feel both fear and shame about them. I hope that those of you who may recognize yourselves in what I describe here may then be able to feel a relief in the knowledge that you are at least not alone, but that there actually are several of us who share this reality.

Another hope I have is that you who read this but *don't* have similar difficulties – with memory, among other things – may still be able to gain an increased understanding of what it can be like to live with such a condition. That we all are different, and many of us therefore don't fit into all these frames the surroundings so often consider obvious, right and "normal". Frames which I, for example, have used violence on myself in my attempts to fit into. And especially to caregivers, I would like to say that now is high time to *really* start listening to what your patients have to say – if you have not already done so – and try to see things from a slightly different perspective. It is only then, I believe, that increased knowledge and understanding really can emerge. For although we live in the same world, we are far from all living in the same reality.

Introduction

"What does it mean to lack autobiographical memory?"

How do I answer that question? When I got it addressed to me, I was once again wholly unresponsive. Yes, I felt like I was empty inside, and that even though I also have been thinking about the issue for so many years. It is so difficult to answer, by which I mean not only in concrete or theoretical terms but also from a more personal perspective. Yes, it is rather more challenging to take on seen from the latter, I would say, at least for me, because the answer then becomes so emotionally painful.

It has now been a couple of weeks since Nouchine asked me the question, and my memory of the meeting itself has already started to blur at the edges, but this feeling of emptiness I still bear with me to some extent. Because I always do.

Part I

1

To lack autobiographical memory

"Memories, even bittersweet ones, are better than nothing."

Jennifer Armentrout

"What does it mean to lack autobiographical memory?" The well-known feeling of fear and embarrassment quickly followed the emptiness that immediately appeared when that question was asked to me, for this is a question that both scares me and makes me feel very ashamed about myself.

I feel ashamed that I don't remember people who meant a lot to me, who I both have liked and been liked by, in a way that I probably should do. Ashamed not to remember significant events in my life, whether they were filled with joy or sorrow. Especially if these events were also important to other people in my immediate surroundings, such as deaths, accidents, births, baptisms, confirmations, or significant holidays and family events in general.

As I now muse over the question, I also begin to fear that I might be wrong. And that fear is accompanied by a shame that I may be telling lies and complaining unnecessarily, especially as there are people who have much more severe memory difficulties than I have. I cannot for sure know how people around me remember their lives and what they have been through. Maybe it is not that much different from what I experience? Perhaps I just imagine that I have a genuinely deplorable, bad autobiographical memory? Perhaps I remember my life without understanding it, and maybe just turn a blind eye to something I can actually see?

I think that the latter fear is almost absurd, yet I cannot entirely dismiss it. Especially since people around me, including caregivers, usually seem to have such a hard time not only understanding what I am describing but also believing that it might be true. It is so easy to begin to doubt oneself and one's experience when no one else seems to see or understand it.

But *I* can see that other people seem to have access to their memories in a completely different way than me. I can be absolutely amazed and even a little jealous – yes, I must unfortunately admit that – when people describe various events they have experienced, and how detailed these descriptions can often be. But what fascinates me the most is still what they *look like* when they tell me this, because it is usually clear that something happens within them when they think back on what they have been through. And *that* is truly something I would like to experience myself.

So, despite these doubts, fears and a rather harsh and punitive superego, I, therefore, dare to say that the fact remains: I don't have access to a functioning autobiographical memory. Okay, I don't *entirely* lack one, but it works miserably poorly, to say the least. And it is also not just that I don't remember certain parts of my life. No, this difficulty in creating, storing or perhaps recalling memories is something that continues to this day, even though, for example, events from last week are at least slightly less blurred than those that took place a couple or three months ago.

What I experience could be perhaps best described as if, for some reason, I were pulling a large eraser after me, which slowly but surely wipes away my autobiographical memory traces. Or at least huge parts of them.

On the few occasions that I have tried – and still try – to tell about my difficulties, really struggling to find the words to describe both how badly I remember what I have been through and how bad I feel about it, I have often been waved away by those I was talking to. As if a bad autobiographical memory is not something to worry about. There is no real understanding, and instead, I often get a pat on the back in the form of words like: "But dear, *no one* remembers everything they have been through in life". When I get such a reply, I understand that I have failed to explain once again, yet I still don't have a good answer to how I should do to succeed in conveying this message.

If I just say straight that I cannot remember anything from when I was in a specific situation, I get, for example, the answer that since I just told that I was there, then I obviously can remember *that* anyway. To continue to struggle with trying to explain that *I know* that I have been there, but just as damn cannot *remember it*, can unfortunately often feel quite meaningless. To try to explain that there is a big difference between *knowing* and *remembering* – at least for me. *To know* is just a factual memory like any other, and it might as well be about someone else. It does not *feel* like an autobiographical memory, because it does not resonate in the body.

I have often tried to describe it this way: What I tell about my life might as well be what I would tell about the life story of a character in a novel; knowledge about facts I have memorized from a book, and therefore something that does not feel either alive or real within me. And although I still have access to a lot of facts about my life – like where I have lived, gone to school, what I have worked with, important events in my family's and my own life, etcetera – these bits and pieces of facts are, to say the least, diffuse and meagre. And lots of the parts are also just missing altogether.

The life stories that I have available and that I am trying to hold on to are in an unstable equilibrium, resting on very few fact pillars placed a little here and there. These pillars are surrounded by huge black areas that I risk falling into if I am unlucky, or when the energy to keep all in balance is not quite enough. And I probably don't need to point out that this is a scary situation to experience, to say the least.

Suppose that I were also to try to describe the diffuse and scanty traces that I have access to. Then my knowledge would perhaps be best likened to tattered, black-and-white photographs of very poor quality

– unlike the (good) autobiographical memory's large 3D prints in colour, with emotional background music.

✉ ✉ ✉

I don't know how many times I have been asked when this memory problem began, or at least when I first noticed it, but the answer has undoubtedly not changed over the years and at the time of writing, it is still the same: Unfortunately, I don't remember. The only thing I can say with certainty is that I have it today and that I believe that it is nevertheless a problem I have had with me since childhood, at least to some extent. I cannot piece it together logically otherwise.

But I can read in my psychiatric medical record that I have thought about this and sought answers at least since the late 1990s. And since I can also read there that I started going into therapy in the early 1990s, it probably means that I became aware then, if not sooner, of my difficulties in some way. Going into therapy without talking about yourself and what you have been through should not work well, I mean.

Although the shortcomings in my memory thus cover my entire life, I have noticed that there is still a distinct difference between my memories – or rather my knowledge – from before and after the age of twelve. Before that dividing line, I don't have access to any memories of my own, but only to knowledge based on information that others have told me. After that, however, I also begin to have access to information that can only originate within myself. But sadly, it is still not memories like the ones I really wish I had access to. Essentially all of them – if not even all – are only diffuse *I know that*-memories.

✦✦✦

I understand that all this can be difficult to understand and imagine if you don't have any significant difficulties with your own memory. I myself have a hard time imagining what it would be like to *have access to* a good autobiographical memory, even if that achievement is probably easier for me. Because, after all, I have access to a pretty good semantic memory. Meaning that I have a memory system that I can at least use as a comparison.

On the other hand, I find it difficult to understand why this problem is usually waved away so lightly. Is not one's autobiographical memory worth more than that? Is it not something that is important to have access to? Yes, it is, but most people don't seem to be aware of it. They don't think about it further, but only take it for granted because it is available.

2

What is autobiographical memory?

"Memory is the diary we all carry about with us."

Oscar Wilde

Before pursuing, I must try to describe and understand what an auto-biographical memory actually is. And primarily how *I* define it, because I am not sure that even memory researchers entirely agree on how our various memory systems should be divided and referred to.

However, whatever the case may be, it is clear that we possess many different memory systems, that I took the liberty of briefly describing in a very simplified figure on the next page, where the dotted arrows are my own musings (explained in the following pages).

First, memories can be divided into explicit (or declarative) and implic-it (non-declarative) memories – where the explicit ones are those that are deliberately recalled, as opposed to the implicit ones that don't need any conscious recalling. Both explicit and implicit memories can then be divided into short- and long-term memories.

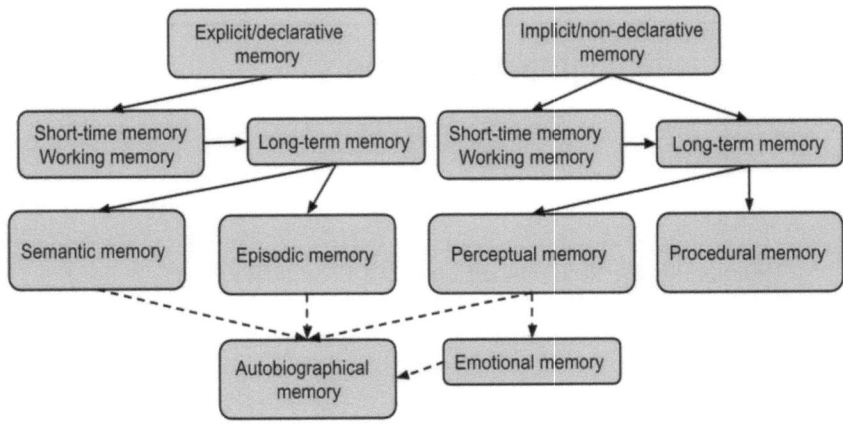

Figure 1: Different memory systems and how they can be divided, where the dotted arrows are my own musings.

Before memories can be sent to long-term storage, they must first be processed in our short-term memory. That memory works constantly, so working memory may still be a better term. Only part of the information is then passed on from here. Most of it is only temporarily used when we need it; things are registered only briefly and then forgotten. However, only information that we pay attention to is processed in short-term memory, so some implicit memories can actually take a shortcut into long-term memory, as we can, for example, encode (store in) impressions unconsciously.

Regarding the difference between working memory and short-term memory, memory researchers certainly don't seem to agree on either the names or the definitions. Some believe that working memory and short-term memory are the same thing, while others think that they are separate. But because the line between them is so fluid, researchers have, to my knowledge, not been able to agree on what an exact division would look like. For simplicity, I am therefore considering them as broadly similar and use these two terms as if they were synonyms.

The implicit long-term memory includes perceptual and procedural memory. Knowledge about how we perform different things is stored in procedural memory, such as riding a bicycle, swimming, tying shoelaces, etcetera. On the other hand, in the perceptual memory, information that allows us to identify objects and orient ourselves in the outside world is stored, together with memories of different sensory impressions, such as visual and auditory impressions, tastes and smells. Thus perceptual memory helps us recognize, for example, a chair and a table and understand what they are to be used for, or allows us to both recognize and recall the taste and smell of, for example, an orange.

Therefore, shouldn't emotional memories be considered as part of the perceptual memory? Because our feelings are experiences of biological changes in our body, along with our thoughts and our way of thinking. Or, to put it in the words of neurologist Antonio Damasio: "A feeling is the perception of a certain state of the body along with the perception of a certain mode of thinking and of thoughts with certain themes."

//

Regarding the explicit long-term memory, a Canadian psychologist named Endel Tulving in the early 1970s put forward his view that this should be divided into two parts: The semantic and the episodic memory, where he, by the latter, certainly meant our autobiographical memory.

Semantic memory stores information and knowledge about everything between heaven and earth. It may be described as our inner reference book for mainly *impersonal* facts. Such as names of countries and people, knowledge of the meanings of words, times of various public events, etcetera. Or why not a description of our neighbour's recent holiday trip. On the other hand, in episodic memory, *personal* facts are stored; information about events and episodes that can be placed in time and space and that are concretely connected to our own experiences. For example, here is much of the information needed to describe *our own* recent holiday trip stored.

Despite the similarities – that they are both something like reference books – Tulving noted that there are differences between these two memory systems in terms of both how the processing of the information is carried out and what type of information is processed. But he also noted an interdependency between the two systems: a new episodic memory is influenced by information already present in the semantic memory. The memory must first pass through the semantic "area" before it can settle down in the episodic "area". And vice versa: semantic memory can bring new information to life through its association with the episodic memory.

When I write "area", it sounds as if our memories would have their very own given place, but that is certainly not the case. Many different areas scattered throughout our brain need to work together to be able to do things that often feel so easy for us.

///

The definition of episodic memory has changed slightly over the years and went from being knowledge of what, where, and when something personal has happened, to also include the actual experience of thinking of oneself in a scenario. Hence for a memory to be called episodic, there is a need for knowledge and awareness that we ourselves have experienced what we remember.

Is not autobiographical and episodic memory the same thing, then? Well, according to Tulving, it probably is, even if he sticks to the more neutral term of episodic memory. But if you look at what some other researchers say, I honestly don't know; there seem to be disagreements regarding both definition and name.

Personally, I have some objections to the fact that episodic memory is considered an explicit memory, even though I am well aware that episodic memories can be deliberately recalled. After all, such episodic memory also contains an awareness that it is something that we ourselves have experienced, i.e. that it is associated with some kind of feeling, whether conscious or not. And it is also accompanied by an emotional charge, whether we can recall the feeling along with the memory of the event or just remember how we felt when the event took place. Moreover, it usually also includes the memory of some sensory impression, such as a sound, a taste or a smell. So should not autobiographical memory instead be placed in some borderland between explicit and implicit memory?

And if you compare the terms – episodic and autobiographical – I think there is a huge difference between an episode and an autobiography. Biographies of our lives contain so much more than just the episodes that we can recall. Such as when and where we were born, and various facts that others have told us about how we have been as people and what we have been through. Things that we don't remember ourselves but still include our life stories. So, even though the definitions largely coincide, I still think that autobiographical memory is something a bit different: It is a memory in which feelings and episodic, semantic and perceptual information are mixed together. But in autobiographical memory, there is also the awareness that this is actually something that we ourselves have experienced. An awareness that gives a feeling, a kind of resonance in the body.

//

One characteristic of autobiographical memories is that they may differ in the degree to which they resemble copies or are reconstructions of the original event (Cohen, 1996). We can thus remember events from an observer perspective or from a field perspective. When we recall the memory from an observer perspective, we stand in the audience and see the event from a distance and can thus better reflect on it. If, on the other hand, we recall the memory from a field perspective, we see the event as when it occurred, that is from the perspective that we had when we were there in the middle of the action.

Observer memories cannot, therefore, be copies of the original event; they must be reconstructions. While field memories are more similar to copies, and hence also tend to be more vivid. Usually, the fresher a memory is, the more resembles a copy, i.e. a field memory. In contrast, older memories over time increasingly take the form of an observer memory. If it is a really emotionally charged memory, it is most likely that it is also seen from a field perspective, and this is especially true for traumatic memories.

/ / /

It may have to be pointed out that what we are talking about here are events that we remember. Of course, but still. For it is the fact that most of what we do and experience every day, if it does not go entirely without a trace, it is in any case only registered briefly and then dismissed to the land of oblivion. These experiences never even become long-term memories. There are actually very few events that we consider worth saving as autobiographical memories, and what helps us determine that relies on our feelings. Because feelings and emotions are an excellent memory glue.

What is also worth considering is that in addition to the "ordinary" ability to create – or whether it is about recreating – autobiographical memories, some individuals have extreme variations of it. Like those (very few) people who have a real super memory and can talk about what they have done almost every day of their lives. This is called hyperthymesia or HSAM (Highly Superior Autobiographical Memory). And recently, it has also been discovered that the opposite condition exists, which is called Severely Deficient Autobiographical Memory. People with SDAM instead lack access to their autobiographical memories, even if they have a well-functioning semantic memory. One can undoubtedly say that I have a version of the latter.

//

We collect most of these memories in more general category groups and place them during different times of our lives. Such as our earliest childhood, school days, family or work life, etcetera. Details are, therefore, the first thing that gets to meet our inner eraser. What remains is a more general picture with a certain, albeit weak, perhaps even unconscious, emotional charge.

Say, for example, that we are given the task to try to imagine a ride we had in a car. We don't remember all the details of either the car or ourselves, do we? Or all the details of everything that was around us? No, most likely, we can "just" recall the feeling around such a journey in general. If we found it pleasant or stressful to drive, if we would have rather sit next to the driver, or maybe we had preferred not to go at all because we easily get motion sickness, etcetera. The car ride that may still stand out a little extra, and that we remember better than this one, is the ride where something out of the ordinary happened, which made us feel more than we usually do on a regular drive. Maybe we saw a collision or were ourselves involved in some accident. Yes, we might even have collided with our future partner, etcetera. Because feelings and emotions, as I said, are excellent glue.

Speaking of the fact that details are usually the first thing being forgotten, it is actually a very clever product of our brain: not to memorize everything, but instead categorize and bring together in different groups. Of course, we can often be a bit frustrated when we cannot remember certain details in different situations, but the opposite would probably not feel very good either.

To continue on the car theme: Remembering all details could lead to the fact that when we, for example, need to make a quick idea of what a car is, we would run into the risk of getting caught up in some endlessly feeding memories of all the cars we have ever seen – size, colour, brand, model year, etcetera – but also of the different situations in which we have seen them, instead of just quickly painting a more general picture within us. Personally, I was now thinking of a money-devouring block on four wheels.

This ability to categorize and generalize also means that we can think abstractly and thus are able to, for example, understand more easily the meaning of metaphors and allegories, that I have such a fondness for. This is something that a person with a more extreme detailed memory may instead have difficulty doing. There is even an expression of just that: "Not being able to see the wood for the trees".

Therefore, it is good that we forget as many details as we do because otherwise, we would find it difficult to grasp what is really important for us to remember. And it can be anything from everyday little things, like the fact that we had decided to meet with a friend or what we needed to shop, to what is actually most important to us – namely, what ensures our well-being or even our survival. Then details are often less important; instead, it is good enough that we remember how something has felt for such memories to be able to guide us in the future. Whether it was boring or fun; painful or pleasant; threatening and intimidating or offering protection and comfort, etcetera.

For example, if we read several fantasy books or saw similar films and liked them, we then have created memories that can quickly guide us the next time we want to buy a book or see a movie. And if we felt bad when we went to various amusement park attractions or in some vehicles, it will later remind us that it may not be worth the effort to try it again. Or we may have experienced something really nasty on our early (or late) jogging, which then makes us choose to exercise at a different time next time.

///

But to return to observer and field memories, it is probably true that memories are *usually* seen from a field perspective when they are fresh, to then increasingly move on to being seen from an observer perspective. For most of us, it is probably still easier to first remember how *we ourselves* experienced the event – what we thought about it, felt, etcetera – before we can then also begin to reflect on the event in general and what was happening around us. Then perhaps we can even think about how other people may have experienced it all, and thus be able to re-evaluate our own experience and change the memory somewhat.

However, it is clear that there must be exceptions here too, and when I think about it now, I am actually one of them. For example: At first, I only tried to recall the memories of the traumatic events that I experienced from an observer perspective; then, I increasingly tried to move on to a field perspective and then also incorporate the feelings I probably felt at the events, something I would rather not have to do again; finally, I would retake the role of an observer, allowing me to reflect more easily on what had happened.

What is described here is mainly about very emotional memories, both negative and positive ones, but what about the more neutral ones? Well, I am myself probably always trying to see what I experience from an observer perspective, and may even have a hard time doing things differently. I am an observer who tries to figure out what is going on around me. And who then also tries to see more of how other people might experience the whole thing, rather than put effort into figuring out what is really happening within myself. Something that is not very successful all the time, but I will return to that later. If *I* do so in most situations, is it unreasonable to think that many other people are doing something similar with at least more neutral experiences? Neutral memories are also the most volatile, the easiest to both change and erase.

///

Our memories change over time. They are actually changing a little every time we recall them, because the new knowledge and experience we gain over the years also affects our memories. And even the emo-

37

tional state we are in at the moment affects the memory we look back on. The fact that our memories change like this can make them a little deceptive. But at the same time, this change is usually to our advantage because we ourselves are also continually changing, and memories may need to change somewhat to fit into our current life situation. Our memories should help us. It is not we who should adapt to them.

When it comes to really painful or traumatic memories, this ability to change is absolutely fantastic, as, over time, we may be able to look back on these events without being tormented as much as when they were fresh. Yes, those memories may then even strengthen us when, for example, they give us knowledge of what we have managed and been able to cope with. Naturally, this change also applies to positive memories, and if we have experienced something really gratifying, we will probably first remember it from this more exciting perspective. But such feelings usually don't last very long and will therefore not do so in memory form either. So when the euphoria has subsided, we will probably find it easier also to remember other details of the event.

Memories can naturally also be changed in the other direction, since we really want to stick to what has been positive and pleasant. For instance, our parents tend to remember how much joy we gave them and how happy and talented we were as children, and they don't like to talk about all that must have been very stressful. Many events may not have been really as fun and exciting as we would like to remember them, but instead, we probably have for various reasons pimped up the memory a little more as time has gone by. A good example is how the little fish we caught on the holiday just seems to get bigger every time we recount the event.

3

Do we need autobiographical memory?

"Everybody needs his memories. They keep the wolf of insignificance from the door."

Saul Bellow

Then why do we create autobiographical memories? Isn't that unnecessary and a waste of brain resources that would be better used here and now, in order to be able to face the future? Do we have access to memories of our past just to be able to indulge in a moment of navel-gazing when we have some time to spare? Or to be able to look back and remember travels and other exciting experiences we have been through, when there is nothing of interest on TV? No, surely we could not have been enriched with such an advanced memory system if it didn't have more essential functions than that.

In 1951, the author William Faulkner's well-quoted words were published: "The past is never dead. It's not even past." That is the case, and with the help of memory researcher Pontus Wasling, whose book contains many illustrative descriptions, I can line up several examples of why our memory is so important to us.

✳ ✳ ✳

Scientists seem to agree that the most critical reason we create memories is to better adapt to the future. However, since the future is already here when I write the next word, we can add that they also help us in the present. We use our experience to handle all the different situations that we are exposed to daily. But we also use our memories to plan for tomorrow, for the future we will experience, whether it is a future that we really want or one we would rather not have.

We create images for ourselves – that we can call "memories of the future" – of what is to come with all the knowledge and experience we have already gained, and update these images when additional knowledge and experience are added. Our autobiographical memories are thus reused continuously, but they also change slightly every time we use them. However, we must not forget that memories are so much more than just what we remember of various life episodes. Yes, skills, learned habits and feelings (unconscious or not) are probably still what governs and affects us the most.

But our autobiographical memories also have great significance for us in many other situations. For example, they help us to produce a picture of who we are, or consider ourselves to be, and how we fit into our surroundings. They also help us create a feeling of an "I". But on the other hand, we surely also need to have access to the sense of "I" in order to create autobiographical memories. A bit like: *Which came first, the chicken or the egg?*

Our life story ties us together with the past. Yes, our memories can perhaps be likened to roots that extend right down to our childhood, where they anchor us and give us a foundation to stand on. And since we also use our memories to construct images of the future, they also help us feel that our "self" is continuous and persistent throughout life, even though our lives and stories are constantly changing.

They also help us picture *other people* and how they might behave, think and feel, based on past experiences from similar situations. Autobiographical memories can also help us in our interactions with others in concrete terms: how many conversations with others do we actually have during our life that don't involve any kind of exchange of memories? If any at all?

Listening to other people's life stories is something I like very much, as they really enrich my experience. Such memories and stories exchanges also lead to stronger ties with other people. Sharing our experiences, listening to someone's confidences, and being listened to in return, not only implies that we get to know each other better but also results in stronger trust between individuals.

Somehow, we seem not to be satisfied with access to our own memories alone, and most of us just want more. Yes, we all seem to have an insatiable need for stories. I'm far from alone in enjoying other people's stories, whether in spoken form or in books that I enjoy reading so much. And the stories don't have to be only exciting or offer to get to know other people. No, they can also help us in practical terms. They can be instructive in many ways; we can, for example, learn from the experiences of others and thus avoid having to make the same mistakes ourselves.

♩♩♩

We are all well aware that life consists of both ups and downs, and that it might be precious to hold on to any positive memory, for when we are down there in one of the valleys. When we feel bad and sad, it can certainly feel good to be able to think back on something that might make us laugh, or at least make us smile. Okay, that it may not cure us, but it can at least cheer up the moment, which can often be good enough.

What if, when we are sick, we could not at all bring up the idea that things will get better – and here I don't mean any progressive disease – what if we could not think: the fact that stomach flu is ravaging me now does not mean that I will spend the rest of my life lying here in the bathroom. And surely, can having access to memories of people we hold dear be comforting in many difficult moments?

Unfortunately, there is also a problem here, and that is that what memories we "choose" to recall are so much affected by the emotional state we are currently in. So when we feel awful, it can sometimes be almost impossible to catch up with any positive memory, because our brain first looks in that part of our memory bank that contains memories of when we were in a similar state of mind. Instead, we need to more actively try to direct our thoughts to a more positive part of the bank. And when we are stressed and anxious, even the ability to recall memories declines, even if they are in there somewhere. Therefore, it may be that we have encountered a powerful physiological barrier when we sometimes cannot think positively, as when we experience depression, which somewhat gets us stuck in a vicious spiral of negative thinking.

♦♦

Memories simply permeate – well, of course it is not so simple – our whole life whether we are aware of them or not, so naturally they are important. But as with everything else, the motto "moderation is the key" also applies here, because neither is getting caught up in the past nor chasing too intensely for good "memories of the future" good for us.

It is not precisely pleasant or constructive: to constantly relive painful memories, dwell on sad events and old wrongs, or remember the good but too stubbornly stick to the idea that everything indeed was better in the past. Nor is it helpful to almost run our legs off in search of excellent education and accommodation, or exciting experiences and travel, or perhaps happiness. No, it is important not to forget about trying to experience what is actually happening to us here and now. To try to live in the present.

How is it then for me? Have I missed that information? Perhaps I am stuck in the past and dwell on "old cupboard food" over and over again when I would instead have to live in the present and look forward? I have certainly heard it said, or at least implied, countless times by people I have met in psychiatry, for example.

Of course, I carry both trauma and difficulties that I return to in my thoughts, but I disagree that this is a matter of dwell. The fact that I am still thinking about episodes and events in my past is because I mainly don't remember them (yes, actually), and therefore, I try to create some sort of images of them. But I also try to understand and sort out some kind of order in it all. However, I cannot deny the fact that I seem to be stuck in *certain* events. Because, even though I don't remember the actual events anymore, my body retains a lot of what I have been through. Emotional memories have been created that are slightly buzzing in the background, and sometimes even make themselves known when I least expect them, when they come back in some kind of flashbacks.

Or at least something like that. I have been thinking about whether everything that I previously called flashbacks should really be called that. Naturally, I believe that some events I experienced have created just such flashbacks. But then there are all the events and in particular the sounds that I have been exposed to on so many different occasions and for so long periods of time (even years) – and specific sounds seem indeed to be the most efficient trigger for me. So when *these sounds* or something like them appear, the anxiety, fear and stress I feel should perhaps instead be labelled as conditioned feelings? In any case, I still believe that it is about some kind of post-traumatic stress, yes even more so: about a complex PTSD (c-PTSD).

4

Traumatic memories – or memories of traumas

"Joy's recollection is no longer joy, While Sorrow's memory is a sorrow still."

Lord Byron

I have often both heard and read that it must be nice not to remember painful and difficult events, but it is not that simple. Even if we don't remember them, harrowing experiences can stubbornly remain in the body, as whole or fragmentary emotional memories, and sometimes come back as flashbacks during which we feel again the same as what we did when the event took place. But distressing experiences can also persist under the form of constantly painful worry and anxiety, albeit so faint, perhaps even unconscious. I firmly believe that the latter form is – but above all has been in the past – how I experience it. I seem to be in a constant state of alert, on guard, trying to avoid being surprised – which I of course end up being anyway – by the terrible and painful feelings and emotions that may arise.

But even the fact that I *don't remember* adds to this constant state of anxiety and stress. Yes, it may be the most crucial cause nowadays as I have managed to process many traumas to at least some extent. And here I am thinking not only of not being able to remember my *past,* but also of my inability to create clearer *"memories of the future"*. To not being able to imagine myself in the future is terribly anxiety-inducing! But I will come back to this a little later.

So what should we do, we who are tormented by such states of anxiety and painful flashbacks? Is it even possible to bring about any change? Yes, I know it is. Because even if I am still tormented by them sometimes, it is not nearly as bad as it was, let us say, thirteen or fifteen years ago. No, of course, I don't really remember how I felt at that time, but I *know* it is true, mainly because I have access to my medical records.

Today my flashbacks are extremely rare, at least in their purest form. However, I can unfortunately still encounter them as fragments – or I maybe should instead call them conditioned feelings. For example, I can sometimes get stressed and anxious by certain tones in voices that remind me of my mum's illness. But I am affected even more strongly by things that remind me of other painful situations I have experienced in mainly psychiatric services. And that even though I don't even remember the situations any further.

Otherwise, the most common fragment variant over the years has been of the kind that reinforced feelings that were already present for some other reason. Therefore, it may have seemed that I have sometimes overreacted in certain situations or that the reaction has even been inexplicable. But it should be added that these reactions also have been due to other difficulties I have – probably even to a much greater extent. And people seem to find it difficult to understand that I can feel so distressed about some situations, such as surprises, changes or too much hustle and bustle around me. Or most importantly, that I don't always understand the situation, the surroundings or even myself properly.

##

Here it is presumably relevant to insert that there is a big difference between a traumatic memory and the memory of a traumatic event. A distinction I have to admit that I myself have been careless about until I now write these words. There are likely many words and expressions we use a little inaccurately in our daily lives, even though we are well aware of what they mean.

When a traumatic memory is recalled, we truly relive that event both in a sensory and an emotional way, as strong as we did when it initially took place, to the point that we can once again become almost speechless because of the strength of the memory. On the other hand, when the *memory of* a traumatic event emerges, we can distinguish between then and now. Therefore, our emotions are entirely different, because they are more anchored in the present and have also been dampened over time. The memory can still be very painful, but then we can put it into words and change the way we think and feel about it, even if it can be difficult. We then have more control over the memory and the feelings associated with it, not the other way around, as what is the case with a traumatic memory. Flashbacks are thus memories or memory fragments of things that we have been traumatized by.

In order to be able to deal with traumatic memories, we must first try to approach them and start daring to talk about them, which may be almost impossible, according to what I wrote earlier. Not only because the associated emotions can be so strong that they make us speechless, but also because we would prefer not to feel them again and therefore suffer the same way again. I would probably never have been able to have a conversation with myself, which I think I can usually do today, unless I had not first been allowed to do it with someone who was more knowledgeable in the field. No, probably I would instead have continued to try to avoid the memory fragments.

Therefore, it is not very successful to put memories in the closet, firmly slamming the door, and believing that we then got rid of them – even though it sometimes may be necessary at the moment, or perhaps it even happens completely unconsciously as it does in dissociation. Nor is it successful to do what I have often tried: to take on the role of a highly logical and distant observer who does not want to feel such things as my own feelings, once I have recalled different memories – or in my case rather knowings – or when in some other way I have been reminded of them. No, sooner or later, those feelings and emotions will catch up with us anyway, so it is probably best to try to grab the bull by the horns. As painful and terrifying as it may be.

I wrote earlier that traumatic memories are recalled from a field perspective, which makes them so vivid, and that observer memories, on the other hand, are reconstructions and thus have somewhat changed. Then surely the logical conclusion is that it would be good to find some way that could help us change perspective when traumatic memories are recalled, so that we can instead look at them as memories of trauma. Because that is precisely what is needed; we must slowly but surely try to learn to look back on the memory from the situation we are in *today*, when we hopefully find ourselves in an entirely different condition to both understand and manage the event better, emotionally speaking.

But, we cannot take this perspective directly. Unfortunately, we first have to plough up the frozen field memory in some way.

/ / /

But what if you, like me, don't have access to memories of the traumatic events, or if they are incredibly diffuse? In fact, I still had (and have) experienced great benefit from talking about what I have been through. Because at least I know that my mother, for example, was ill during large parts of my youth, and I also know what this period as a whole looked like – and a few more specific events – this has allowed me, through logical reasoning, to create myself if not a memory so at least a picture of what it *probably* looked like. Admittedly, it is a diffuse and almost unreal picture, to say the least, because I have trouble both remembering and imagining something, but such an image is still better than none at all. It can also be added that the picture is most likely embellished; the reality was probably much more frightening.

Sadly, I have also felt terrified in my contact with psychiatry, and thus creating traumatic memories and memory fragments from the long time I have been a patient there. Yes, the fact is that I have become much more traumatized by some of my contacts with psychiatry than I ever was by my mother's disease. Sad but true. And I don't mean the contacts I had with psychiatry *because of* her illness, but the one I later got when I also decided to seek help for myself.

It was terribly frightening, stressful, and anxiety-inducing to struggle year in and year out to try to understand psychiatry itself, how it worked, and what was expected of me as a patient. And then I felt so incredibly lonely, neglected and unsuccessful when I could not cope with it, and just came to feel increasingly worse. Unfortunately, this has left deep traces that affect me to this day, both in my psychiatry and somatic healthcare contacts. For example, I have found it even more challenging to ask for help and stand up for myself. And I also find it all too easy to put the blame on me and despise myself, when the contact with healthcare is not working properly or when I am being mistreated.

But in any case, these memories are often easier to find out about and then also to work with because I have access to my medical records, and therefore I can more easily piece together different images and scenarios. I have also had the opportunity of processing many of them along the way, because I have at least had access to two fantastic psychologists. However, as if I was damned now again, I have to admit that I feel very great fear and stress when I think about what psychiatry's opinion might be on the reflections and experiences I am trying to share. For perhaps I still have myself to blame in many ways and therefore should not have the right to complain or grieve in this way?

However, I have since been able to – and still do – work with myself by using these images. For example, to learn not only to understand how important our feelings actually are and that we should not dismiss them – something I did in the past and unfortunately still sometimes do – and to better deal with the painful and frightening emotions that sometimes arise. Emotions that are often related to things I have experienced in the past. Because when I can put these into context, I can also more easily reconcile myself with them; I find it easier to deal with what I understand. So over the years, I have slowly but surely become a bit kinder and fairer to myself, both when different feelings and emotions appear and when something does not work as it should or even goes completely wrong. For example, I no longer take sole responsibility for the ignorance and shortcomings that actually exist in healthcare. Or at least try not to do it.

♩♩♩

Even though my flashbacks have become so much fewer and easier to handle, they still exist to some extent, and even more difficult to wipe out are the feelings I have now instead chosen to call conditioned. What makes these seem so sustainable?

When we experience something that is really hard, something really painful or scary, and then don't get the chance to process the event properly – including during sleep, which is often disturbed after a frightening experience – we can suffer from something called post-traumatic stress disorder (PTSD). And then flashbacks, but also recurring nightmares, are common. It is about memories that seem to have frozen in time and space. The various emotional memory pieces have certainly been saved in, as I believe, the perceptual memory where they belong, but there they then spin around in an eternity loop. And the strength of these pieces has not diminished over time, as it usually does, but are as strong as at the time of the event.

Unfortunately, such memories can then permeate our entire life: We can be anxious and continuously stand in a kind of readiness; if we have access to detailed memories, in addition to having flashbacks, we may also avoid situations that are in the least similar to the original event; if we don't have access to details, we can still be surprised by flashbacks and then constantly worry about new ones, also avoiding places where they appeared. And sadly, we may even start to look at ourselves in a completely new way. We can create a very negative self-image where feelings of shame and guilt can become both strong and pervasive. Something I am unfortunately too aware of and actually often struggles with to this day.

If I now have it all reasonably clear to me, then in various areas of the sensory cortex (in the brain), has been created what Antonio Damasio calls representations for the different impressions that we were exposed to during the traumatic event. These representations then lie dormant until a stimulus triggers one of them, then also triggering the others. In this way, the entire emotional machine can be started once again and move us back in time to when the event took place. We experience "the same" strong feelings that we did then, or maybe even stronger because we may also be afraid by the fact that we are experiencing this flashback. And this can then happen time and time again when we encounter triggering stimuli, and that with undiminished force.

I can describe here a really powerful flashback I experienced sometime during 1993–1994, when I was admitted to a psychiatric ward, and which I can retell because I have done so several times since the incident took place. The event itself I otherwise have no memory of anymore.

At the time, I was trying to rest in an armchair in my room – which was easier said than done as the hospital stay was pure torture for me – when I suddenly heard a sound that made me fly out of the chair in panic, rush out of the ward, take the lift down the eight floors, rush out of the hospital, out of the hospital area and run down to a small lake located a bit away. I am no longer really sure if I also ran around it, which could perhaps be about a couple of kilometres, before I even stopped and began to reflect. Or if it was probably rather the case that I then slowed down and walked (or jogged) around it, while at the same time trying to figure out what the hell had happened.

I don't know if I understood the context myself or came up with it together with the attendant I used to talk to at night. But in any case, the sound I heard was of a head hitting the hospital's stone floor – a woman had fallen or thrown herself down – and it reminded me of when my mother had been sick and done similar things.

At first, I probably could not at all understand why I overreacted in this way. I who always tried to keep the mask on and instead was usually stiff with fear. But I imagine that this particular fear made me run as far as I did before I even could reflect on it all. A sound had triggered a previously experienced fear in me, which then in turn opened the floodgates for the fear I was feeling about the situation I was currently in, namely a terrifying hospital environment and the fact that I didn't seem to understand either psychiatry or myself. I guess I got scared by the fact that I was afraid, and that caused me to start running and so on.

♪♪♪

How can that be? As I wrote in the introduction, memories can be divided into explicit and implicit memories. Where the latter are the ones we recall unknowingly – or of which we may never even become aware – and which must therefore have undergone some unconscious encoding process as well. Had that process instead been conscious, we would have been able to put the whole thing into words and thus also be able to recall the memories consciously, as we can do with the explicit ones.

The implicit memory system develops before the explicit – which is perhaps quite evident if we consider, for example, that we don't talk until the age of two or three – and is actually active already in the fetal stage so that we have access to implicit memories when we are born. Just think of how newborns can recognize both the voices and the music they heard when they were in their mothers' wombs. And like to be rocked.

My mother told me that she was really on the move all the time when she was pregnant with me – there were, for example, two large dogs who needed their exercise – and that as late as a few days before my birth, she was cleaning and sweeping to make the flat nice. Yes, she was both scrubbing and baking. My parents had also bought me a nice cradle, which is something they then came to regret. Because once I came into the world, I wanted to be rocked all the time; my father even learned to rock me in his sleep. It took me a while to get used to not wanting to be on the move to settle down – and when my brother came into the world three years later, the blocks were already in place under the cradle.

And it is not just that we already have these own encoded implicit memories with us when we are born. No, thanks to evolution, we also have access to "memories" (or instincts) created earlier than that since they were required to protect our survival. Consider, for example, the suction and grip reflex that young children have. It's also about "memories" created to protect us against various threats and dangers, and then quick reflexes can really be life changing. For example, we get scared and back off when something big comes toward us or when something very suddenly appears in our field of vision.

Therefore, it has been of utmost importance that our brain found a way to be also able to encode and store memories that don't depend on either our attention or our language skills.

✳✳✳

Most implicit memories are created and built up by being exposed to a stimulus several times or by doing something over and over again, that is, through a certain number of repetitions. Therefore, the encoding and storage of such memories usually take a much longer time than that of explicit memories. But once done, these implicit memories are also tough to erase, unlike the explicit ones that need to be recalled and dusted off sometimes in order not to fall into oblivion entirely. Think, for example, of all the kings and their reign dates, or all the lakes and streams we were once taught in school; surely we don't remember all of them today?

But as I said, there are exceptions when it comes to such (implicit) memories that are created to protect our survival and well-being. Just think about how quickly we learn that we should not lay our hand on a hot plate once we have done it once. Or when it comes to such experiences that are really painful and frightening for us, as in the case of various traumas.

In the vast majority of situations, the two memory systems work side by side, and therefore we can also put into words what is happening. But in traumatic events, it can work a little differently. When we experience something – for us in particular – really terrifying, special survival measures may need to be taken to prevent us from perishing. Because if a situation makes us feel completely overwhelmed, if we feel both threatened and completely helpless, well, then we naturally focus first and foremost on survival. Then we usually don't have the ability, strength, or opportunity to simultaneously put into words what is happening, and therefore also risk getting stuck in this eternity loop.

Then, what needs to be done is to somehow move on from here, as it obviously is not a "normal" autobiographical memory. Because even though some people can remember the event in great details, it is still the strong feelings that are in focus. Feelings that reason cannot control, although we *know* that we are no longer in the threatening situation. For many (including me), even details can be entirely missing or be very sparse, and then it is just a terrible emotion that sometimes appears as out of nowhere. That it can be terrifying to be surprised in that way, and not really know either what it is due to or what it was that triggered it all, is perhaps not so difficult to understand?

In my case, the painful emotional memories don't even seem to have been appropriately integrated with any other memories of the events; they seem to live their very own lives. Although other people may have access to most of their memory pieces, they can persistently spin on in the same (survival) track. Even though it may have been several years since the event took place and they are no longer either threatened or helpless. So what then needs to be done is to organize all the memory pieces, save them in the two memory systems, and reduce the emotional memory's strength to a more manageable level to create a more normal, even though painful memory. We have to create an explicit memory that we can put into words so that we can also start to talk about it, and so on.

In typical cases, this happens to some extent when we sleep. Because then our brain encodes important memories for us, but also forgets parts that are not so important to remember. During what is known as REM sleep – when we dream – our brain processes the emotional events we have experienced, and does that in a state without stress, thus allowing us to release many of the emotional charges associated with them. The volume of emotions is reduced so that in the future, we don't experience as strong feelings every time we remember various events, or in some other ways are reminded of them.

But sometimes this does not work. Even though our brain does its best by perhaps even dreaming about the traumatic event over and over again in the attempts to process it and deal with all the pain that we have experienced. But instead it will just be a constant repetition of the trauma in the form of nightmares. We may then need some help, and one form of therapy that has been shown to be very effective in traumatic memories and PTSD is the one called EMDR.[1]

///

I will not linger on the fact that I may also seem to get caught up in events and episodes that are *not* about something directly traumatic. And yet, fine, I will admit that I just cannot stop myself from thinking about things that I don't understand, and especially if they are important to me or those closest to me. The thing is, I just have an *enormous* need to understand and sort things out. Once that is done, I can (usually) put it aside. Or perhaps instead incorporate the knowledge with what I already have access to. For example, I may need to talk and think about situations where people have acted, reacted or expressed themselves in a way I have a hard time understanding. And the same goes for situations where I have a hard time coming to terms with

---

1. See appendix for more information about this form of therapy.

what I myself have said or done. In other words, things that others often consider to be trivial and apparently just something to shrug their shoulders at. I seem to find it easy to get caught up in all the "whys" I had even as a child:

– Why is that, Mum?
– Why do they do that, Mum?

5

Living in the present

"Yesterday is gone. Tomorrow has not yet come. We have only today. Let us begin."

Mother Teresa

And what about the present? Well, since I am really stuck in just that, I can describe it, and it is not nice at all. I often feel as if the present has taken me hostage. Or if I tried to put a slightly more positive spin on it: I got the lead role in a remake of *Groundhog Day*. And once I truly stop and try to get close to the meaning of that fact, both mentally and emotionally, the words "terribly frightening" fall extremely short of describing it.

Not only is it scary and sad, but I am so incredibly ashamed to be as stuck in the present and with so many routines as I actually am. And to have such difficulties, not only when it comes to breaking these routines, but even just to change them slightly. It is not that *I cannot* do it, but it is complicated. Yes, it is almost impossible for several of them to tell the truth.

///

There are, of course, several reasons why I have such a great need for routines. And I think some of them are not due to my memory problems but to other difficulties I have, which also affect, among other things, my imagination. For example, the routines give structure to my days and help me save both time and energy, since they allow me to avoid constantly being faced with choices that might otherwise get me stuck for way too long. Or even shut down completely.

I would find it hard to get anything done if I constantly had to make different decisions – which in my case would result in over-analysing and over-thinking things – based on me and my own needs, as my inner compass does not seem to work too well. Without this compass – or in other words: without proper access to my feelings – it is difficult to find my own path in life, and therefore it can be good to have at least access to routines. This makes me think of a few lines in one of Iris Johansson's books, where she describes something else that I can recognize myself in. Because I also make sure that I always try to create or take on various projects or assignments that I can deal with, which can lead me forward. Both big and small.

"The worst is for us who are autistic, because we have no idea whether there is any way to follow. It does not come from within us, but possibly we can turn something into a mission, and that is what I live on."

In addition to the directives and requirements that accompany the projects I engage in myself, I can also take on other people's assignments. Following others' demands, wishes, and needs are often much easier than listening to my own inner self, as they are often stated clearly and distinctly. Then I usually have no significant difficulties in either knowing or dealing with what needs to be done. But instead, one problem that can then arise is that I risk getting hurt myself and sometimes even being exploited, because I so much want to do the "right thing" and please others.

Like several other activities, the routines are also anxiety-suppressing, partly because when I focus on them, I can more easily avoid thinking about what my life looks like and the various difficulties I have. Having access to well-known routines also creates a kind of security and a nook for me to rest in, because then I know what to do and what this in turn leads to. For me, it is anxiolytic and calming to know that after A comes B and then C. And the peace I find in rituals and routines can thus often give me the energy I need in order to be able to deal with the more uncertain elements of the outside world again.

Although my memory problems may not be the only reason for my need for routines, I am convinced that they play a huge role. For both the fact that I have, to say the least, major problems with being able to imagine the future, and carrying experiences related to both my mum's illness and my contact with psychiatry – that so much is difficult to understand and that nothing can be really safe and can also change in an instant – mean that I have a considerable need to have something safe to hold on to. Something that is not as unpredictable and uncertain as both life and people otherwise often are.

Hence I need to continually try to stay one step ahead and kind of nibble the track for myself, in order to try to avoid painful surprises; or to be left in anxiety because I don't know either what to do or where to go. Or risk stepping straight into those black areas without memories or even knowledge that I wrote about earlier. Or risk making mistakes in front of other people and then run the risk of revealing my difficulties to them as well. In other words, things I want by all means to avoid.

✦✦✦

Avoiding. Well, it often feels like I am doing nothing but just that. I avoid: thinking about the traumatic events I have been through; that I don't have a functioning autobiographical memory; that I then also lack a well-functioning ability to imagine the future; that I'm so damn dependent on routines, and also that I have a hard time breaking them to at least create new ones; that I don't really know and understand what all my difficulties are due to; that I have no job; that I have no social network... And there are probably more things that I avoid that I cannot think of right now – maybe just because I avoid them.

Even the fact that I avoid so much makes me feel great sadness and fear. And so much shame, of course. I can often accuse myself not only of not being able to have the strength to look the truth in the face, but also of not just getting my act together and making sure to overcome all obstacles. To make sure to be a well-functioning human being.

So if we look at how many different situations during which I seem to experience these very feelings, and the fact that I even do so in the face of my way of functioning and the various difficulties I have, it is perhaps possible that other people also think that these feelings best describe me as a person? But I really don't hope so, because I always try to think positively as far as possible and at least outwardly seem happy.

Over the years, I have found many descriptions in books written by Elisabeth Rynell that fit me exceptionally well. And then I mean above all in terms of how I *feel* in many different situations. When I now wrote this about avoidance, getting stuck in routines, fear and shame, I realized that there are a few lines in one of her books that I really think fit in here. Because in addition to feeling like a failure, I too often feel just like a coward.

"I would like to know what I am so afraid of. I am always afraid. There is a dull desolation that eats me. There lies the horror rolled up, like a potted plant leaf that has fallen on the windowsill. I will take detours. I close one eye."

"Sitting still is the only protection I know of. While I sit, I have time to think a lot. I often accuse myself of this very silence. That I am so cowardly. I am my own cage."

"I had never imagined that life could be like this. As a child, I was quite happy, it is said. I can probably seem happy now too. Maybe I am even happy, without knowing it. "

In order to really value the present in the best way, we probably also need to have access to our memories. At least, this is how it feels to me. Because without my memories, I feel like a leaf in the wind. But I also feel like a prisoner of the present and of the routines that I need to stick to. Naturally, I *can* value many moments that take place here and now. But there is still always a background feeling lurking and disturbing me, as a constant, albeit weak state of anxiety and stress. And that even though I really do my best to avoid that feeling.

I wrote earlier that it is probably partly related to the traumas I have experienced. And also to the difficulties I have when I am in contact with other people, and the fact that I don't even understand myself properly. But of course, the feeling is likewise constantly present due to my great memory difficulties. It is both frightening and stressful to have neither proper access to my past nor the ability to paint a clearer picture of the future. And even if I manage to value the moment, let us say a trip, I can still not recall the memory of it later, at least not as others seem to be able to do without any problems.

6

Living without autobiographical memory

"A life without memory is no life at all"

Luis Buñuel

Naturally, it is not as bad as the quote above states it. But I undeniably feel very alone about living without an autobiographical memory as it is a problem I rarely hear anyone else talk about. On the contrary, I get to share other people's autobiographical memories continually. Something I personally don't mind as I really value being able to take part in these conversations. I have not managed either to find any description that I have really been able to recognize myself in in the non-fiction literature, but have only come across descriptions of people with immensely more significant difficulties than I have, for example, due to major injuries and diseases of the brain, or severe dissociative disorders.

The loneliness is not diminished by the fact that I am so ashamed of having this problem. No, the fact that others seem to have such a hard time understanding means that instead of sharing my difficulties, I do everything to hide them – even from my own family. Sadly, this means that I can sometimes feel very lonely even when I am with them. Because when we talk about our shared history, for example, I become aware that I don't have access to the memories they carry with them. I then often barely participate in the conversation but only nod and mumble in agreement or take on a more passive audience role. It can be very painful to watch my family when they are in that shared memory room, a room that I don't have access to. Even though it can sometimes be full of sad memories, I nevertheless have this damn desire to find a door through which I could also enter.

Unfortunately, the fact that I hide my difficulties also means that I feel bad in another way, because I can feel like a big liar when I talk about or behave as if I actually remember. And I feel anything but good about dealing with untruth. So it can be quite challenging to talk about me at all, but even more anxious is when I sometimes end up in situations where I am expected to talk about events that I cannot even imagine, even though I have obviously been present. I mean events I not only lack memory of, but have not even managed to create an image of myself by previously having talked about them, read about them or at least seen some photographs taken from them. I can therefore admit that I don't take much pleasure in, for example, meeting an old classmate in town.

***

Why, then, am I so ashamed of this and feel such a great need to want to hide it? Well, first and foremost, because other people seem to have such a hard time both seeing and understanding my difficulties at all, it makes me even doubt that they even exist. Then, in addition, when I still sometimes try to tell and describe how it really is, I often get misunderstood, or worse: not believed at all. Is it then so hard to understand that it can often feel easier to just continue to hide it all? I am not only ashamed that it makes me feel different, but also like a failure in some way. And who wants to feel that way? This can be very painful since I still have a longing to be understood, and that also in terms of many other difficulties I have.

And since it is easier for us to remember things that we are interested in, maybe that means that I was not interested enough when it comes to, for instance, larger and more important events in my and my loved ones' lives? At least others might see it that way, which to me feels terribly shameful and frightening.

But what I am most ashamed of is still that I don't remember people in a way that I probably should. And then I think especially of the people who stand and have been close to me, and who can be or have been very important to me in many different ways. I am not only ashamed of having great difficulty remembering, but also really feel a great shame over myself. Over the person I am, or at least I seem to be.

I can feel a great fear that I must be a nasty person, I who don't re-member these people, or at least cannot imagine them in a vivid way, because one says that we remember those we truly love and care about. And must that not mean that I am a pretty horrible person, one who can neither love nor care for others? However, that is not the case; I genuinely care about other people and I also constantly try to do my best to show it in different ways. But maybe it is often in the wrong way, as I usually want and can better, help and support in a more practical way? Although I am actually pretty good at listening too.

So it is not just that I lack memories of the moments I have spent with someone or our shared experiences. I just don't remember the person. I don't mean that I have forgotten that they exist, but I cannot paint an inner picture of them, or at least find it *very difficult* to do so. Now I don't mean primarily a visual image, which I otherwise lack the ability to paint, but a mental image of their personality, my feelings for them and their feelings for me. Therefore, when the person is not present, I find it impossible, or at least extremely difficult, to recreate the positive (or negative) feelings I can experience when we are together.

But when I then meet the person again, I will, of course, remember them, although I may need to make an internal update of their personality if some time has passed since we last saw each other. And it can actually be about such short periods as just a few, single weeks, if I don't know the person very well. Here, however, it can be added that, for example, telephone contact can mean that this time without updating can at least be extended somewhat – but unfortunately, I also have a pretty hard time with telephone contact.

/ / /

There are so many people I no longer have any memory of, and several of them have even been my family members. What does it really say about me? I have no memory of my grandmother, who died when I was eleven years old. Nor of my father with whom I had my last contact when I was fifteen, or any memory at all of my family before the age of twelve or thirteen.

After that, it becomes instead diffuse *I know that*-memories in different strengths: from super-extremely diffuse recollections to memories of the fact that my brother and his family are at least there now. I only have a very vague knowledge of my grandfather, who died when I was 21, even though I used to meet him very often and liked him a lot. And now, after my mum's death, even the memory of her has begun to become somewhat blurred, even though it has only been three weeks since it happened when I am writing this. Words cannot describe how terribly frightening this all feels, but writing these words really makes me feel physically ill!

Naturally, I also feel a great sadness that it is like this. Because it means that I cannot really imagine, for example, the pleasant feeling of both liking and being liked by someone when the person is not present. Sadly, this means that carrying someone with you inside, and that that when you feel bad, for example, you can be comforted by the thought of someone you love, does not work so well for me. Although I can often try to hold on to and feel good about *knowing* that someone likes me, believes in me, and so on.

It also feels infinitely sad not to be able to remember all the lovely moments I must have experienced during my childhood, and which my mother could often describe very vividly. Like when she was standing there with freshly baked pancakes, for example, when I came home from kindergarten with all my artistic creations, or how she was continually trying to answer all my "whys?". Or like when my brother and I very happily (and messily) munched on her freshly baked muffins and rice chocolate cakes, or snuggled in our reading corner under the stairs, or took a cheese sandwich and hot chocolate in the self-built snow hut.

I would also so very much like to remember what it was like when we met grandma and grandpa every weekend. And also how it felt to later, as an adult, sit and talk to him, a person I am said to be very similar to and whom, as I said, I liked very much. And I would desperately like to be able to remember what it was like to hold my lovely niblings in my arms for the very first time.

In addition to this grief, I can also often feel a very painful mixture of great feelings of shame and guilt, because I cannot remember all the good moments that I still *know* that my mother and I had together. Because instead of helping me get hold of and recall all the memories of all the nice things she did for me and with me during my childhood, for instance, or all the pleasant experiences and journeys we also had and made together as I got older, my body sometimes still only comes dragging with those less pleasant and diffuse emotional memories created due to *her illness*. I want to be able to remember *my mum* and the lovely person she was. Not her damned disease. Here I feel that a strong expression would be appropriate, because this is indeed very painful!

///

It is said that clues of various kinds can make it easier for us to grasping our memories, because recognition is easier than recollection. And that being in a state of mind similar to that we were in when the events took place also can help. So some excellent clues should then be, for example, photographs. Not to mention returning to the actual locations of the events, or at least to some similar environment.

But that does not either seem to help me, not much anyway. As I said, I can feel terrible in hospital environments – and then mainly the psychiatric one – and also in the presence of students. And I can also get very sad when I hear some of Kate Bush's songs as I probably often listened to them when life was very hard. But I guess that is pretty much it.

Needless to say, I have turned and twisted photographs in trying to remember something, but the only thing they are capable of is creating *a knowledge* that something has happened – which in itself is an asset to me – they don't help me *remember* it. Photographs can also scare me. For instance, many years ago, when I was putting together a slideshow DVD for my mother, I found pictures from a trip to Germany that we had apparently made with my brother and his girlfriend. A journey that I then had no idea about, and yet I had been the one who drove the car.

Many years ago, my psychologist took me on tour to the various places where I grew up and went to school, but even that didn't help my memory in the least. And when we later talked about our shared trip, I had even begun to lose my memory of it – and today I don't remember it at all. And going by (by bus) the flat I lived in between 1991-2000, twice a week on my way visiting my mother until her death, didn't make me remember what it was like to live there, nor what it looked like. A flat in which, for example, my brother and his girlfriend told me that I (for the first time) would become an aunt, and where I must then also have been visited by my newborn niece. Great events for me that should hence have been worth remembering, I would say.

So all this fills me with infinite fear, shame and sorrow. The only thing I can hope for and try to hold on to is that I myself probably suffers the most from it. After all, other people don't know that I don't remember them in a way that I should probably do, but hopefully feel that I like them and care about them once we meet or when I am showing it in some other way. But I really cannot help but often curse my brain for, for some reason, seeming to have adopted the saying: "Out of sight, out of mind".

♦♦♦

I now have described how many of my memory difficulties can manifest themselves and also how I feel about it all, but if I should yet try to sum it up a little better. And then both in terms of how significant the shortcomings in my memory actually are and how it affects me daily in different ways. But also try to describe how, with the help of different strategies, I still do my best to deal with these shortcomings and difficulties and hide them. I think that I can start here with the examples I previously presented about why our memory is so important to us, and based on them, then describe what it looks like for me.

But first, I should still start by describing what my life as a whole has looked like. Partly to try to show how poor my autobiographical memory is, and partly to see if I can find answers or clues as to why I have these memory problems and the other difficulties I have. After all, psychiatry has always insisted that the answers to most questions about why I function as I do are in my upbringing and my relationship with my mother. Something I myself today don't consider to be the case at all, but sadly likewise tried to believe for so many years, and that even though at the same time it made me just feel worse.

So with this description, I would also want to convey how wrong it can go when you don't consider how a patient might function fundamentally. That there may be biological reasons why a patient functions as they do. Symptom relief is, of course, good, but even more important is trying to find the root of the problem. Yes, if you don't know about it, you risk hurting the patient even more with the relief you offer. And for me, knowledge has also been what I have most wanted to get hold of. Knowledge and understanding are indeed a strength for me. Because if I have it, I usually also get access to how I can handle various problems and difficulties in the best way.

Part II

7

My life and my contact with psychiatry

"You never know how strong you are until being strong is the only choice you have."

Bob Marley

Growing up, school and work

As I wrote earlier, I don't have access to any memories whatsoever from before the age of twelve. So I have no memories of either what it was like growing up in my family, playing with friends in the small community where we lived, or what it was like going to kindergarten or primary school. No memories at all of any Christmas evenings, birthdays, holiday trips, school days, school graduations or school trips, etcetera. And then, of course, no memories of all the people I met and socialized with, or even lived with, during these years.

But I have been told that I was a smart little girl – have been called precocious – who was calm, confident, happy and very curious, and who also cared for other people. My mother has described it as if I was born an "adult", and thus I was incredibly easy to care for and wanted to do a lot myself. I was apparently so calm, confident and difficult to provoke that even at school, I was placed next to more agitated children because I probably had a calming effect on them as well. But I can see in photographs that I also seem to have been quite tough and confident, something of a "tomboy". And I have also been told that, for example, I decided that I would become a doctor when I grew up and nothing else, even at a very young age.

♦♦♦

We have already stated that strong emotions are an excellent memory glue, but not even these seem to have helped me to get memories from these years to stick. For example, my brother was very ill – had severe febrile seizures, among other things – and hence there were many frightening scenes with both hospital stays and ambulance trips. Yes, once even his life hung on a very fragile thread because of *me*, when I, unfortunately, happened to hurt him by accident. It was apparently a very nasty event, with a lot of blood and travel to the hospital in a hurry where I myself was glued like a postage stamp in the back seat of a taxi.

Then my grandmother died very suddenly when I was eleven years old, which was probably a very disruptive and painful event for both my mother and the rest of us. My mother has told me that I was in the hospital shortly after her death, and also that we later gathered at the chapel and said goodbye and sang for grandma once she was in her coffin. According to my mother, this was a very nice and peaceful moment that touched both my brother and me in a very positive way, but sadly, I have no memory of it. And as I said, I don't have any memory of my grandmother from when she was alive either.

About six months later, my mother apparently lost consciousness when my brother and I were alone with her. And while my brother then quite understandably became hysterical and thought that she too was dead, I instead tried to convince him of the opposite. And I also dialled the number of my mother's friend and asked for help. But none of this, or the many other *very* emotional events that also took place during these years, seem to have strengthened my memories in the slightest. Something that, for me, feels both strange and unimaginable.

///

My father had difficulties and a personality that probably didn't make him particularly easy to live with. At least my mother got very hurt by it, and when I was twelve, my parents divorced. It was also at that age or just before that I, in a way, took the big step into adulthood. Because then, I started to support my mother in many different ways and also became something of an extra parent for my brother. And when she later became ill, I even came to take over her role as the adult and parent in many situations.

After the divorce, my brother and I moved with our mother to the small community where she had grown up and where our grandfather lived. I then had the opportunity to meet him very often until he died when I was 21 years old, but I don't have any memory – apart from a very diffuse knowledge – of either him or the things we did together.

❀❀❀

My mother got sick when I was thirteen. And sadly, that disease then permeated substantial parts of my life – and naturally also hers – with psychosis, intermediate manic and depressive states, and in between my own stress and anxiety about what could possibly come next. Of course, she was not sick all the time, and there were many pleasant periods during the years as well, until I left home when I was 25 years old. But I still think that for me, it led to something of a constant, albeit often weak, state of stress. Especially since, at the time of the divorce, I had promised myself to really try to take care of and protect her properly.

Sadly, my mother didn't have any insight about her disease, so at every psychosis relapse, it was necessary to try to get police assistance to get her admitted to the hospital, using the Compulsory Psychiatric Care Act (LPT in Swedish). It is something that is definitely not easy to do, either literally or figuratively, and my mother, myself and my brother all suffered very severely from it. I know I always felt terribly distressed about having to let my mum down in this way. Having to expose her to something she didn't understand she needed and didn't feel good about at all. And further, having to send her to a hospital ward that was indeed awful in many ways. Even once in the hospital, it would take several weeks before she realized that I was just trying to look after her best and wanted her well after all.

So it is no wonder we all came to feel so bad about her illness. And I myself have carried not only pain and fear inside, but also a lot of guilt and shame because I felt that I should have been able to protect and support her better. I also had such bad feelings when I thought that her illness and needs were stressful, especially if I also said it out loud, in a way that was as if I had thought or spoken ill of her. So I even feel guilty when I write these lines.

Unfortunately, my brother and I didn't exactly get much support from psychiatry. No, quite the opposite. Instead, they were probably often grateful that I was as strong and competent as I were, and hence could solve so many situations and support my mother. In this way, they usually got away very easily.

I know that my psychologist later told me that the counsellor had had a bad conscience that they had not tried to do more for me during my youth. And when I had admitted myself, I was told by a chief physician that they had often wondered in meetings how I had actually coped with everything at home. Both comments that I don't know today whether to laugh or cry about. Then why didn't they help me? But at the same time, I wanted to take care of my mother in the best way, and I probably managed that, except for the medications, usually much better than what psychiatry did. Because, understandably, the ward in particular was pure torture for her.

I still have some memory fragments – albeit extremely rare now after my mother's death – from this time, in the form of flashbacks and something similar, an increased level of stress and anxiety and sometimes nightmares. But otherwise, I essentially don't remember anything at all. It is only diffuse *I know that*-memories, which are also very few in number.

✶✶✶

In addition to the stress caused by my mother's illness, this move also meant that I was now probably beginning to feel that something was disturbing in contact with the other children and young people my age. Something that also certainly made me feel both stressed and anxious. But at the time, I probably just thought it was related to the fact that *my situation* – being a divorce child with a sick mother – was slightly different from theirs. Not that it was *I myself* who was different as I know today that it actually was. Even during these school years and the years to come, I was usually as cool as a cucumber, something that my classmates obviously had some fun about. I know that I got the nickname Ferdinand (the Bull) in high school because it was probably tough to get me upset. At least outwardly.

I don't remember much more from my lower secondary school days than that I know that I thought it was not easy. Mainly because the school was located in the community we lived in, and therefore, my classmates knew a lot about what was (outwardly) happening in my family. Consequently, I had to put on a mask and play many various roles during this time and try to fit in as best I could. Taking so much responsibility for my family and home and not being particularly tough and cool, but more of a bookworm, was probably not something that most other teenage girls easily accepted. And then I got a little teased about it, too.

Of course, I had to keep the mask on even when I started upper secondary school, but since that school was elsewhere and I also got new classmates, it was probably easier to at least hide my family situation. Something that was also positive was that the classmates most likely thought I had friends at home, and vice versa, so then it must have been much easier for me to find excuses to be able to withdraw. It was easier to hide how comfortable I thought it was to stay at home and how much responsibility I took for my family, but also to hide how terribly uncomfortable I probably felt with my peers. Moreover, it was now ideal to be a bookworm because that would almost be the case when you had chosen the programme I had done.

But how much do I remember from my upper secondary school days? Well, pretty much not much more than what I have just written now. Thus, a *knowledge* of how it probably felt but without any further details, and so a minimal number *I know that*-memories. I don't even remember anything from my graduation other than I know it was tough then. To this day, I thus feel some distress to see and, above all, hear students, so I try to keep my distance at that time of year.

✦✦✦

I have no real memories of what it was like in my home and with my family, or how it later became when my mother got sick, apart from the ones I previously talked about and some very diffuse nightmares. Nor do I have any from my school days; no memories of either events or what the rooms and premises looked like. I don't have any memories of the trips I made with my mother and my brother either, even though the most memorable ones took place in adulthood. But perhaps I should try to see that from a little more positive side, because today I could actually visit Jersey, London and Paris, for example, and experience it as if it were for the first time.

If we consider the role of feelings and emotions again, my cousin and I, for instance, travelled to Spain for two weeks when I was 21 years old. Nothing I wanted to do but I went after pressure anyway. It is a journey I have absolutely no memory of, and that even though our grandfather sadly passed away while we were there. Unfortunately, I don't remember grandpa's funeral and everything around it either; the only thing I *know* is that my mum felt very bad about all this.

To take a positive emotion instead, my brother won a lot of money the year before our grandfather's death, which must have been a great experience for my whole family. Yes, both my mum and I truly tried to do our best to make him feel as good as possible, despite the difficulties we had in the family. And so, this then 17-year-old boy played and won this huge win! It must have just been so significant for all of us! But of course, I don't remember that either.

///

After having had some odd jobs and also failing to start my studies at Lund University – the transition was simply too overwhelming, and so was the social part – in 1989, I got a job as a night porter in a hotel in the city. That was when I truly realized that I had difficulties in contact with other people, and I probably could not turn a blind eye to it anymore. When I moved to my own flat in 1991, unfortunately, my life's stress got even worse, instead of better as I had probably anticipated it would be when I would finally start focusing more on myself and my own issues.

But it was not only the contact with other people that became increasingly stressful here, but so did the work itself. Often it was so unpredictable because there were constant changes, and most likely, this was also purely sensory overload for me. Thus, the job was very varied and sometimes very stressful and probably toiled at me quite a bit. But at the same time, there were also advantages as I had to take care of myself to a large extent at night, even though the working hours themselves were very stressful.

Of course, I could not do much about the changes that arose, but I know that I did my best to deal with the unpredictable. And I think it was something my colleagues had some fun with. When I was a new employee, I always walked around with a large notepad where I wrote down the answers to the almost infinite number of questions I had, so that I then had something to rely on in different situations. If that situation arises, what do I do or say? If computers or phones are malfunctioning, how do I solve it? If guests behave this or that way, how do I deal with it? Yes, I can imagine that I was considered inquisitive, to say the least, but to be prepared as far as possible for both the potential and the almost impossible, is my way of trying to suppress the anxiety I so often feel when faced with an uncertain future.

But although I worked at the hotel for a few years, I hardly remember any of that either, and it certainly feels very strange. After all, it was my first, more proper, permanent job. One that I was also good at and where both employers and colleagues also valued me. Yet, I have only a knowledge of the work in general and a few isolated events. For instance, we made several trips together, and today I would especially like to remember the one when we went to Berlin, as it is supposed to be such an exciting city.

Because the work was so social, it also meant that I got a lot of new contacts, colleagues and friends. That is why I started to struggle more and more with really trying to get active on many different (social) levels. But unfortunately, it didn't always work out so well. At least *I* didn't feel good, because I didn't seem to fully understand or cope with contact with my colleagues and friends as well as I wanted to. Something I became increasingly stressed and sad about.

So both the difficulties in contact with my colleagues and the work itself meant that I was now just going to feel worse. I know that over time, I felt so bad that I even vomited before I went to work as I didn't know what was in store for me there. I became more and more anxiety-ridden and depressed, and now I also had an increasingly clear eating disorder. The latter's funny thing is that it was actually through a colleague and friend that I learned that you could vomit after eating. Something I had not even thought about before; I had only been comfort eating. I had now also started drinking some alcohol – I who had barely touched a drop before – both in my attempts to fit in better and for anti-anxiety purposes.

I had great difficulties, but when I later received a sickness compensation (pension) and resigned from work, I still got an excellent recommendation letter. And it shows how good I can be at just hiding how I feel and how I function. For example, I cannot really do many things simultaneously, but since I often work very fast and am good at focusing on one thing at a time, it can probably still look like I do. The fact that I can actually be – and often am – very stress-sensitive will soon become apparent here in the text, although I can obviously at the same time be quite good at hiding it. Well, I certainly often am something of a paradox.

"As a night porter, you do the nightly work at the reception with computer work, finance work, telephone exchange and ongoing reception work such as check-in and check-out and customer invoicing. The job requires that you can keep many balls in the air at the same time, work independently, take your own initiatives, have a high level of stress and a distinctive sense of service as well as computer knowledge.

Malin has always been dutiful, loyal and very meticulous in everything she has done. She has done all her duties in an excellent way.

When Malin now, after a period of illness, ends her employment with us at her own request, I wish her all the best in the future. She has my warmest recommendations!" (Reception manager)

As I said, it was during these years that I also moved to my first flat, with all that is involved. And the first move usually makes a significant memory to most people, does it not? At least I thought so. Then, in that case, we can now state that I must be the exception that confirms that rule. But I probably carry some emotional memories with me from this time, because now it started to be very painful to fail in my interactions with people. Yes, even failing in my friendships.

It was at this time I sought help from psychiatry, more specifically, at the end of 1991. Not for my memory problem, which I may not yet have been fully aware of, but in the hope that they might be able to help me understand what I was doing wrong, so that I didn't feel comfortable with either my work or my colleagues. But also hoping that they could help me better understand how other people function, what they most likely consider and think in different situations. Besides, my colleagues had obviously started commenting on how thin I was and nagging me about my eating. Something I became increasingly scared, stressed and sad about.

Hence I contacted the counsellor I had previously met in connection with my mother's illness, who, after my move, had promised me that I could get in touch if I ever felt the need to talk. Here the first – there would eventually be many of them – unpredictable and painful change in my future contact with psychiatry arose, when the counsellor then sent me on to a psychologist instead. Something I absolutely didn't want, but still agreed to because I probably felt that I neither could nor dared to turn down the offer.

Then my very long and painful journey began. Sadly, a journey that would become something of a downward spiral, where I would only feel worse by all the changes, all new contacts, and my constant attempts to fit in and do the right thing. And then, at the same time, trying to take care of and understand myself, understand my surroundings and the psychiatry, and what was really expected of me. Sadly, something that I realize psychiatry had difficulty seeing, but perhaps above all, difficulty understanding.

Gunilla Gerland perfectly describes the feeling that in the coming years would now only grow stronger within me. A feeling that I regret to admit that I struggle with quite often to this day:

"It had to be my own fault that I failed at everything, that I had no life. The will to live had withered in me. I hadn't the strength to wish for anything any longer, except possibly to be away from everything."

The contact with psychiatry begins

The psychologist was certainly competent, but I can see in the medical record that she had her sights set from the start, that she thought she understood me and my problems. According to her, among other, my problems mainly had to do with my mother and her illness. Then, of course, I too began to think that this must have been the case and started working with myself from that point of view. I was assessed to be "neurotically structured" and therefore began to attend an insight therapy treatment twice a week.

Now all of a sudden, my life became even more uncertain and changing. And there were also a lot of balls to try to keep in the air for me: I should be a good daughter and support for my mum, but also a good sister for my brother; I had to cope with a stressful and very social work; I should be a good friend and colleague; I should try to be a good patient with the psychologist, but also with the district doctor to whom she had, in turn, sent me.

It says in my medical record that I was increasingly depressed; that I was increasingly affected by feelings of guilt and of being unable to live up to the expectations of others; that I got an increasingly critical view of myself; and that I also physically became increasingly worn out due to my increasing eating disorder and my alcohol intake. At the end of 1993, my anxiety and stress finally became utterly overwhelming, and I simply could not take it anymore, either physically or mentally. This is when I agreed to be admitted to a psychiatric ward and be on long-term sick leave. A sick leave that after a few years would be changed into the sickness compensation (pension) I still have today.

✸✸✸

This first admission turned out to be as long as ten months. Something I hardly had expected the day I first walked through the door. It was also not something I actually wanted to do, because my psychiatry experience was certainly not the best, and I also felt terrible in that environment. But naturally, I still followed my district doctor's advice. So now I found myself in another difficult-to-understand, unpredictable and challenging environment, with many new contacts that I had to somehow try to understand and relate to. I must have been outright terrified. And felt very, very lonely.

"Is very tense during the conversation, laughs a little embarrassed often. Cannot agree to that it is nice that she has finally come here, but probably intellectually

Even in the ward, as I see it, they came to focus on the wrong things. Or at least *assume* the wrong things, namely that my distress and difficulties must stem from my upbringing and my relationship with my mother. Yes, that I too sooner or later would become a patient with them was probably almost something they had expected, because as someone there said, "we first take care of the parents, then of the children". So here I was supposed to try to allow myself to feel bad, to try to get closer to my own feelings and needs, so that I could mature in that way that would make it easier to be in contact with others.

The paradox is that in my medical record, I can see that many of the needs I have are being described as almost pathological. Something I also knew or felt. Having to withdraw, not being able to cope with too many people or changes, and needing routines and rituals, for example, were things I should try to change. The word "afraid" is now also starting to appear more often, which in itself was correct as a description of how I felt most all the time, but it still gets so wrong when it is used to describe how I feel about people.

"It is very difficult for Malin to form new relationships. She is afraid of new contacts, afraid of being in a group. Preferably working for herself, is very meticulous, picky." (Doctor)

The difficulties that I felt were taking place when I was in contact with other people should then naturally try to be solved by being exposed to more people, something I, among other things, had the opportunity to do there in the ward. I would practice feeling confident and "dare" to expose myself to more situations, such as those mentioned above, through contact with staff and fellow patients. Although I made good contact with a few people – especially with a night attendant who came to mean a lot to me, a woman I then continued to have telephone contact with even after my stay – the gods should know that I felt anything but good there in the ward and would have preferred to discharge myself. But...

"At the same time, she feels she cannot do that, has no other option. She would not be able to explain to [the psychologist] and [the district doctor] why she had discharged herself." (Doctor)

//

Apparently, yet both the ward and my psychologist saw the stay as something positive, and that the fact that I was feeling worse was perhaps more of a sign that I was starting to lower my guard slightly and begin to approach my feelings. And then I tried to see it that way too, I guess.

A little sad, I think, that I seem to have thought that all these painful emotions that were now starting to arise inside me would only have been something positive, when I should have understood that this was not the case. That much of what psychiatry thought was right for me was instead even harmful, and that I really should not have kept pushing myself like that all the time but should have said "Stop!" sometimes. But even though I later actually tried to do just that, it didn't happen; but instead, I came to continue to push myself for many years.

I am really ashamed that I didn't understand better. But at the same time, I could not know and took it for granted that caregivers were the ones who knew. Besides, as I said, I have great difficulty with changes and uncertainty, so it was better to continue to stick to what I had at least partly begun to get used to – therapy and hospitalization – than to embark alone on something completely unknown. It was a bit like when someone stays in a destructive relationship; you know what you have but not what you get.

"Very ambivalent about being here. Malin goes on to say that the anxiety is sometimes unbearable, and she has to make an effort not to collapse. It is a great challenge for Malin to be here in the ward, but as she endures and then hopefully even grows a bit." (Doctor)

"Malin is informed of [the psychologist's] assessment that the stay here is valuable, gives her security and has 'lubricating effect'." (Chief Physician)

"Malin is fighting to be able to stay here. Perceive this struggle as worthy." (Doctor)

So I just came to feel worse. And now, I had also totally lost contact with my colleagues, which was the reason why I had turned to psychiatry in the first place. The situation was undeniably becoming a little absurd, and yet this downward spiral had only just begun.

I no longer understood what I was actually doing, and according to my medical record, I also found it very difficult to believe in an improvement. However, I still wanted to keep trying, keep fighting. And I did so by adapting to and embrace psychiatry's views on what was probably the best thing for me. I didn't know what to do, so all I could do was try to follow the advice given to me. I was really stuck in a foxhole – and would be so for many years to come.

> "Malin really uses the time here and works with herself all the time. Fighting courageously, purposefully. However, has very great demands on herself and thinks she fails every time she loses control." (Chief Physician)

> "Malin describes her struggle to remember things from her childhood and try to get all the pieces of the puzzle in place." (Doctor)

> "Malin is very tired, hardly sleeps at all at night. A process has begun that she cannot stop. She is being torn to pieces, fighting." (Doctor)

/ / /

I was now also becoming increasingly worried about how my illness affected my mother. Not that I spoke to her about it, but just the fact that I was in the hospital meant, of course, terrible stress and anxiety for her. Otherwise, I showed my distress to neither my mother nor my brother, or at least I tried not to. And this constant jumping between the completely different roles I took on here, and over the years continued to do, also nearly tore me apart.

> "It has been a difficult week for Malin with anxious and messy patients in the ward. She is still ambivalent about whether she really needs to be here. A lot of energy is used to calm her mother, who suspects that Malin must feel very bad to need such a long period of care here." (Doctor)

Time passed, and we had to try to see what my future might look like. Personally, I now felt that I could not return to my work at all. Partly because I felt so horrible and also could not "switch off" in the same way as before, and partly because I felt that I only had the ability and energy to work on one thing at a time: my pain or a "normal" job. And furthermore, I had also completely lost touch with my colleagues. Psychiatry became increasingly frustrated with my situation: that I myself had no plans for the future and didn't know how to move forward. Hence consideration was given to both treatment centres and work trials through the rehabilitation department called AMI.

> "She is having a hard time making up her mind about anything, and according to [the psychologist], she needs to be pushed. As far as future plans are concerned, two possibilities are being discussed. Partly treatment centres in Falköping and partly work trials via AMI. Malin thinks she cannot handle any of them but does not completely refuse, and according to [the psychologist] she can be persuaded." (Doctor)

My concern for my mother became justified because she slowly but surely started to feel worse. Which, of course, meant that I too started to do so. In the best of worlds, surely psychiatry should then have been able to do something to help both of us, one might think. But that was not how it worked. No, when I asked my mother's doctor for help, even when I was hospitalized, I didn't get any. Instead, it would take eight to nine months and several dispatched district doctors – to try to get a medical certificate – before my mum finally came under care. Now the situation in the ward indeed became entirely unbearable for me, so I discharged myself.

> "For some time now, she has noticed a certain deterioration in her mother that suggests that she is entering a psychosis. This feels very difficult for Malin. When [the chief physician] suggests that Malin might ignore the mother and let the neighbours take care of her, Malin immediately protests and says that it is completely unthinkable. Malin also says that she herself wants to draw the

heaviest load to protect her little brother, 'it is enough with two mentally ill in the family'." (Doctor)

"The patient is tense and anxious, reasoning adequately and insightfully about her difficult struggle. Expressing a death wish, however, denies current suicide plans. We are constantly aware that Malin has a very high suicide risk, and the only thing that keeps her alive is that the mother needs her." (Doctor)

"Discharged today unimproved at her own request. The risk of suicide is still high. The whole time of care still does not feel like a failure, but Malin has gone through a large part of the painful process and is now more open than before." (Doctor)

After the discharge, I agreed to try AMI, although I was "very negative and felt as it was one big failure", according to the psychologist's notes. My contact with the psychologist didn't work very well either, as I felt both unsuccessful and like a nuisance. Yes, the psychologist has even written that I "oppose the possibilities to progress". So I ended that contact – but only to come back a few months later since, at the same time, I felt failed to have then failed with the therapy. Something I naturally could not reconcile myself with at all. Because giving up is not something I do in a hurry!

But of course, I also felt awful and was thus in great need of support, especially now that I had started at AMI. And when it was time for work practice, it became so bad that I even decided to commit suicide. However, I could not let my mother and my brother down in that way, not without at least once again trying to find another alternative. Therefore, I aborted the suicide attempt. Instead, I got on my bike and went to the hospital to talk to the wise attendant I had made such good contact with. But if she had not worked that night, I don't think I would be sitting here today. Once there, I was then unconscious and also hospitalized for two to three weeks.

///

I almost don't remember anything about this contact with psychiatry. And that despite the fact that I was hospitalized for so long and felt terrible about it, to say the least. But I know that I constantly felt terrified, failed and stressed by not understanding psychiatry. And also, by not seeming to be able to receive and use the help offered to me, but instead just came to feel this much worse. Yes, so bad that I wanted to give up my life and even tried to do so. So because of all this anguish, some emotional memories have undoubtedly also been created here. For example, I still have nightmares about psychiatry sometimes, and I also tend to blame myself too often when in contact with the health-care system.

Here it can be added that even most of my nightmares are mostly made up of emotions and contain hardly any details at all. Often I wake up totally terrified and very stressed, without really being clear about what it was that caused it all. But I believe that my nightmares are often not even actual recollections of past events, but instead often are more about the present and the future. Something may have happened the day before, and once I lower my guard during the night, it triggers old fears as well, but that these fears also appear to reinforce the fear and anxiety I already feel. But of course, I am not sure that this is the case.

What I have also noticed lately – when I have worked with this text and then started to grasp some details in some of my dreams – is that my brain is now making up entirely new stories. Even though they still revolve around my contact with psychiatry and my mum's illness. So I don't dream about the actual events, which I don't remember, but the old emotional memories are instead connected to completely new images. Which is precisely what our brain does when it creates most of our dreams, I guess.

"The patient is severely tormented by nightmares and sleep paralysis and ends up in a state between wakefulness and dream, where she has all the effort in the world to eventually be able to anchor herself in reality." (Psychologist)

///

According to the medical record, my psychologist nevertheless encouraged me to continue in psychotherapy and "invest in my own development". And naturally, I too wanted to sincerely believe that it might still work out, that I might be able to live up to her expectations and finally succeed in something, so we continued for a while longer. After the AMI failure, I even accepted to get a referral for a treatment centre evaluation. Which I think says a bit about how much I actually fought rather than resisted, as a stay in a treatment centre was both the most terrifying and most degrading thing I could ever imagine. The funny thing was that once I started the examination, I found out that if I were going to get a treatment centre place, I would lose contact with my psychologist. Something I had not understood and that obviously no one else had given themselves time to explain to me either.

"Is clearly ambivalent about the visit here and explains it on the basis that she wants to make [the psychologist] happy. Indirectly expresses a great need for help and seems to be very suffering but has no clear motivation to seek help through treatment centres." (Psychologist)

We have now come to the end of 1995, and I was more or less left like a wreck by this psychologist who was conducting the evaluation. Besides, I was absolutely terrified. It was, namely, only the alternatives of internships and treatment centres that were discussed at the time, and I could not really cope with any of them. But neither could I just ignore everything, so naturally, I was at my wits' end and hence felt extremely pressured. Yet over the years, I would feel even worse, but thankfully I didn't know that at the time.

Naturally, the psychologist saw how badly I felt, but as for the reasons for it, the focus continued to be on my relationship with my mother here as well. Nevertheless, I can see in my medical record that already at the first meeting, when we addressed them, I didn't understand my difficulties in contact with people and then especially my peers. And that I also continued to return to it again and again. So it feels very sad that they didn't put more focus on it. After all, that was the reason why I sought help.

"Besides, the image appears of a person with a character disorder, a very ambitious and meticulous person with high demands on herself and her surroundings and who has developed an insufficiency with borderline traits and where the self-destructive traits are prominent. It is also about a mutual bond between her and the mother and a stalemate that has become after the divorce." (Psychologist)

"She also describes as a problem that she cannot function with people, especially peers." (Psychologist)

"Repeats over and over again that she cannot handle people." (Psychologist)

It was not only myself who didn't want or thought I could manage a stay in a treatment centre, but also the psychologist saw several question marks. Partly my self-destructive behaviour with, among other things, food and alcohol abuse and suicidal thoughts, and partly my age, as I had now reached 30 years. Besides, we had not been able to come up with a common problem formulation on which we could work constructively. Something necessary because it was, after all, a voluntary form of treatment. And indeed, we could not have done so because much of my real difficulties were not brought to psychiatry's attention. Sadly, I myself could not give a proper account either, as I too didn't have full awareness and knowledge of all my difficulties.

After a few visits to the psychologist, I could not take it anymore. So we interrupted the assessment attempt, and I simultaneously cut off the contact with my district doctor. Instead, I had to focus on helping my mother sell her house and move to a flat. Moreover, I was now wholly resigned and no longer had any hopes of being able to receive the help offered to me, and therefore considered myself a nuisance. However, the psychologist didn't give up but promised to get in touch later on by telephone, to see if I actually stood by my decision.

Although this particular move may not be the best example – since it was indeed quite extreme in many ways – it is nevertheless telling for one of my difficulties. Namely, not having the energy for more than one thing, or person for that matter, at a time. Not if I want to solve situations or problems in the best way anyway. Something I certainly always want to do. I want to and need to finish one thing before I can deal with the next one. That is also something that has unfortunately been a little difficult for psychiatry to understand.

Treatment centre or not

Four or five months later, I reconnected with my district doctor, and I also took the courage to return to the evaluation psychologist. I was terrified, of course, but at the same time, my situation was still complicated, and I didn't know either how to be able to live on or whether to end it all. Actually, I could not bear at all either the idea of a treatment centre or the one to now go to the clinic in Falköping again. Or even the one to go out to my mum every day, but somehow I still found the strength to do it all.

> "The patient comes to today's visit and is extremely tense and pressured. Sitting and shaking the whole visit through; and the back of her hand is completely torn and bloody. She also has a greyer complexion than she usually has. The patient performs with great effort and also manages to complete a questionnaire. Shakes very strongly and has pain all over the body." (Psychologist)

After completing the test part of the evaluation and also making a study visit to one of the treatment centres, we were finally able to state what I already knew: that I would not be able to cope. And then a new crisis arose: What would I do when I would be entirely without help, apart from the contact with my district doctor? Standing all alone in a world that had become many times more difficult to understand and uncertain than the one I lived in before contacting psychiatry, when I had at least had a job and colleagues.

Naturally, I was very ambivalent about it all and wanted both help and no longer anything to do with psychiatry at all. An ambivalence that has since kept up with me all these years. And this constant uncertainty, but also the outbursts – I would call them meltdowns today – which would now increasingly occur during changes, for example, came to be seen as that I feared abandonment. Or being "swept away and rejected." Something that was not precisely true, not in the way psychiatry meant anyway. Because it was the changes and the uncertainty itself, not knowing what I was going to try to relate to and adapt to that frightened me. And also the fact that I could not even understand myself properly.

So when I found out in the autumn that the psychologist had both been given permission and wanted to offer me continued contact, even though I would not be in a treatment centre, it must still have meant an enormous relief for me. Okay, I was still completely terrified and incomprehensible, but then I at least got something to hold on to, something that was not *as uncertain* as the alternative. I could then try again to plan for something. Namely, to start visiting the psychologist and try to figure out what to do there. And then hopefully also succeed better than I had done with the previous therapist. I got a new chance to try to be a good patient. Of course, the coming years would now be extremely frustrating and challenging for my psychologist, but also terribly painful for me.

"We are now fighting both of us to find our way to some kind of meeting where we can both endure. The patient shows good will but also that it is very difficult for her, and she can tell me that after the visits here, she feels that she has failed and that she must punish herself." (Psychologist)

"Malin comes more or less tormented and closed every week. Opens up sometimes but then pulls the aisle back together next time. She is full of self-accusations and super sensitive to how I put my words." (Psychologist)

"She is still very busy trying to figure out what to do with me and [the district doctor] to be able to please us, find out what we want her to say and do." (Psychologist)

Not having a clue what I was really trying to accomplish with the psychologist, and the constant feeling of neither understanding nor being able to make myself properly understood, naturally tore me terribly. And so did the continuous switching between the different situations and people I now had to try to relate to, where I had to take on various roles. One in front of my family and then mainly my mum. Another in contact with the psychologist and the district doctor. And a third when I was with myself, when I had nothing to hold on to at all.

Nor did my memory problem make things any easier when I could not carry feelings and experiences with me from one meeting to another. Or with me home, for that matter. Besides, I need time to get hold of my thoughts and words, so it was fortunate that I here still dared to use the letter writing and later also phone calls. It became a way for me to both try to make myself understood and keep the memory of the contact and the psychologist alive.

"The patient is always terrified that I will come up with new suggestions for measures and changes that she feels she cannot support." (Psychologist)

"It is often easier for her to make herself properly understood by letter than in direct contact. It is also very difficult to avoid when you meet face to face that communication goes awry because we often add different meanings to the words and tone. Malin is also extremely afraid of harming with her way of being." (Psychologist)

Since I was getting increasingly stressed and scared and could not get any order at all in either the contact with the psychologist or myself, we decided that we would start seeing each other twice a week. To see if it then could be somewhat easier for me to endure the situation in the meantime. But also endure our meetings, because I was usually so pressured when I was there that I got meltdowns and ran away. This was something I was both ashamed of and despised myself for, which in turn led to both self-harm and even more stress and fear. A downward spiral, as I said.

"After a moment of despair, she does not have the strength to sit still but gets up and rushes off according to previous patterns. She is so tense and has so much pain in her body that she limps before disappearing out the door." (Psychologist)

"However, this arrangement with a patient who has such great contact difficulties and severe anxiety with self-destructive behaviour feels completely inadequate and questionable in the long run." (Psychologist)

Perhaps the psychologist thought that I sometimes overreacted more than justifiably, that I was a bit of a drama queen. But for me, this chaos that occurs in my head when overloaded is something hellish, and then there are only the options act or "switch off" – or meltdowns and shutdowns. Where the latter is the alternative that I use most without comparison, even though, as I said, there were many meltdowns just in contact with psychiatry. Now that I have contact with people with autism spectrum diagnoses, I have finally gained a greater understanding and acceptance of these difficulties. I am namely far from alone in having them.

While closer contacts were good – I also had my district doctor in addition to the psychologist – it was also exhausting to have to switch between different situations and roles in that way. I also had an intense fear that my mother would become psychotic if she found out what difficulties I really had, so I constantly struggled to make it all look as good as possible. Besides, it was now terribly stressful not to know if or when the Swedish Social Insurance Agency might submit a proposed measure. Or even know how long I would actually be allowed to keep my sickness benefit. I was therefore slowly but surely being torn to pieces.

> "Malin is simply finding it increasingly difficult to live up to the level of her surroundings when it comes to socializing, and she is becoming increasingly desperate." (Psychologist)

In the end, the situation became entirely chaotic for me, and I could even imagine not receiving any money at all just to avoid this constant, internal uncertainty. After many crisis reactions, it was therefore decided that I should receive a sickness compensation (pension), which I received in the spring of 1998.

Then I also found out that the diagnosis of emotionally unstable personality disorder, or borderline, had been put on me. (Later, bulimia and generalized anxiety disorder, GAD, would also be added.) Something that made me feel terribly bad and that I actually feel bad about even today. Now I became even more afraid of myself and my difficulties, which certainly didn't make my situation any easier. On the contrary. I could not see that the diagnosis was correct at the time and can even less do so today. Instead, it was a completely wrong diagnosis that would hurt me very badly. But like darn, I now came to try to relate to that very description of my difficulties as psychiatry would probably still know best.

///

In order to insert something positive in all this misery, my brother had a daughter in the summer of 1997. A huge event in our family, of course. In November, as a proud godmother, I also got to stand there with her in my arms when she was baptized, and my brother at the same time took the opportunity to get married. Both events I really would like to be able to remember but sadly don't. And that although I have access to both video footage and photographs. It is both very sad and scary, and especially the video gives me very unpleasant feelings of unreality.

///

In the spring of 1998, I was apparently in such a deplorable state that the psychologist felt I had to be hospitalized. Given my abuse of food and alcohol, she recommended the detox clinic in Falköping. But that was not the only reason. No, we had also talked about how such a ward might be at least a little easier for me, since the staff there probably would not interfere with my mental state that much. Therefore, I might be left alone and thus be able to concentrate more easily on resting, instead of spending time and effort trying to adapt and live up to the surroundings' demands and wishes.

Of course, I didn't want to go there because I knew I would feel awful in the ward, but I still agreed. And one of the reasons was that the psychologist would then let go of the idea of contact with my mum and her caregiver. Something she felt we needed to do, but that I didn't want to hear about at all. But I also wanted to try to make her happy, to be a good patient, because she had now come to mean a lot to me.

Here it can be added that my alcohol intake was never really a primary or chemical addiction. For the most part, it was instead about a routine addiction in the same way as and in connection with my food addiction. But naturally, it was abused anyway and was also used for anxiolytic and sometimes even punitive purposes. On the other hand, we can, unfortunately, talk about both severe addiction and abuse when it comes to food. Also, it is one that I dare say can be much more difficult to get out of, because we actually all need to eat to survive.

Both the psychologist and the chief physician in the ward did everything to make both the admission and the stay easier for me. Something I must have been very grateful for, although I can read that I was both prickly and dismissive. Or, in other words, very stressed and scared. However, I only managed to be there a week before I felt that the whole thing was overwhelming, but I had then managed to get pretty good contact with both the chief physician and the head of department. Always something.

> "It has been with the summoning of all her powers that she has endured, and now it is no longer possible. She has nothing against the ward or the care as such, nor does she have anything against the staff; it is just that in hospitals, she cannot stand being." (Chief Physician)

> "However, she hates herself for not having the strength to stay; she feels it as a failure, which feeling I try to take out of her. On the contrary, I think she has done a good job here." (Chief Physician)

After the stay, I continued to have contact with the head of department for a while. I probably visited him in connection with my meetings with the psychologist and thus was still in Falköping. What was good and right for me in that contact was that he was so tough and straight-forward, something I valued because then I didn't have to think so darn much about any underlying message.

But unfortunately, our contact also ended in a sad way, and it was I who "chose" to interrupt it because, in the end, I could not cope with his often *too* cheerful attitude. I also am humorous and definitely like to joke, but sometimes I need to be serious and thoughtful as well and then it is not always time for jokes. I know I said this to him, and even asked him not to always take everything so lightly because I got hurt by it, but sadly, he didn't agree to it. By the way, he had not under-stood my difficulties properly either, so I would have had to interrupt our contact sooner or later. But this still felt like a new failure.

"The final phase of our conversation takes place in a much cheerful form; after all, the patient has a very nice sense of humour. It is also noticeable that her daily routines constantly guide her. Gets more nervous when the undersigned deliberately drags out the visit." (Head of Department)

///

I continued to struggle with the psychologist and district doctor and also went out to visit my mother most other days. Hence I became increasingly exhausted and frightened when I felt that nowhere did I truly manage to live up to the different expectations and wishes. In fact, I didn't even always understand which they were. If anything, I really would have needed to get a better explanation of my difficulties. Knowledge that I could have embraced and used, because knowledge is the Alpha and Omega to me. Then I would have had something to hold on to, and that had meant that I would at least have understood *myself* better. And I would also not have had to contend so infernally with trying to fit into the social framework that was so wrong for me.

Because I struggled even in my loneliness with trying to adapt to what psychiatry seemed to think was right for me, and tried to understand how I apparently functioned based on their view of my difficulties. For example, I read books about borderline and searched for knowledge I then tried to embrace. And I probably recognized myself in something – or rather thought I did – but felt with all certainty at the same time that there was also a lot that was not true at all. But *what* that was, I, unfortunately, could not put into words.

I can see in the medical record that I could not even understand why, for instance, I was so affected by changes in visiting times or during holidays. That I could so completely lose control of such seeming trifles. Something I truly despised myself for. And I could neither understand nor explain why I so often became both sensory and mentally overloaded and then got these shameful meltdowns. So what I did then was to really try to fit into the diagnosis that had been given me, by "reshaping" me and telling me that this was exactly how I functioned. I namely had (and have) such a terrible need for recognition and understanding.

> "It is thus a treadmill that the patient has to run on and however you do, and however you suggest, it always goes wrong in some way. It ends up with the patient feeling worthless as a human being, daughter and patient." (Psychologist)

> "The patient also beats herself, tears herself in the face and on the body and bangs her head to 'knock the shit out'. The patient cannot accept being a person, and she cannot accept being a person who thinks and feels differently from what she herself accepts within the narrow frameworks she has set for herself." (Psychologist)

> "She is stuck in an impossible situation, where her physical and mental suffering is very great but where also a tremendous sense of duty and stubbornness makes her fight on." (Psychologist)

Of course, I can only agree that I ran like crazy on a treadmill. And I understand how difficult and frustrating it must have been for the psychologist not to be able to help me, and also that it might seem from her point of view that I rejected all attempts to find good solutions. But personally, I absolutely don't think that was what I did, but that I was just trying in some way to survive while struggling with trying to fit into the surroundings. After all, it was not only me who had set up these "narrow frameworks", but also psychiatry had indeed such that one had to try to fit into as a patient.

In another attempt to understand, I took courage and asked if maybe the district doctor, psychologist, and I could meet together, thus trying to ascertain whether we were all striving in the same direction and whether I fought in the right way with both of them. But above all, I was probably hoping to understand perhaps then what they obviously understood about me. Something that I myself had clearly wholly missed.

The meeting evidently went great from their perspective; they got along well and looked at things quite similarly. They also had a "positive attitude towards my chances of moving forward, despite my difficult life situation." But what became a good meeting for them became something of a disaster for me, something my psychologist probably had a hard time understanding.

Not unexpectedly, I don't remember this, but today I have no difficulty understanding that I came to feel so bad about it. Today I can see what probably happened there, and I also see in the medical record that I actually told the psychologist that I felt left out. That for me, it felt like they represented a completely different world, one from which I was excluded. So although I found out that they were thinking along the same lines – something I needed – I also felt that glass wall that I can so often feel when I am with people. The one that makes me unable to genuinely reach my surroundings; that I don't seem to be in the same reality.

This glass wall – the feeling of being in a glass bubble and then looking like I participate in different situations but often still don't – probably also arose very often with the psychologist. It is a feeling that is very painful, especially if you don't know why and therefore cannot put it into words. I also despise not understanding or making myself understood and can become very scared and anxious when that happens. The fact that I often became so panicked in meetings with the psychologist that I had to rush from there, I therefore no longer see as the least bit strange.

> "Says she feels deceived by her parents, deceived by the mental health services and deceived by [the district doctor] and me, who encourage her to feel but then she cannot feel but constantly has to try to switch off, which at the same time becomes increasingly difficult for her." (Psychologist)

> "The patient constantly apologizes for her behaviour, so also this time when she apologizes for, as she thinks, throwing shit at the mental health services at the last meeting. It is very difficult for the patient, and it is easy for us to get our communication wrong even if we try to do our best from both sides." (Psychologist)

> "Is so compulsive in that she has to try to make her mother happy at all costs while she herself is falling apart. We stand and stomp on the same spot." (Psychologist)

I really would have needed to get access to knowledge here. But in order to then also be able to take it to me and work with it in the best way, I would also have needed to have access to a reasonably predictable and understandable world. An environment that, for me, would have felt at least relatively safe and reliable but which had also *understood me.* If I had, I am convinced I would have been a heck of a much better patient and behaved very well. And besides, I would then probably have been able to feel much better myself.

> "Is bewildered now that her body cannot take it anymore; it lets her down even though she beats it all she can. In the past, it has worked, and she has been able to switch off and be able to carry out her duties. The patient is asking today about the medications that we talked to [the chief physician] about a while ago." (Psychologist)

When both body and soul were failing me completely, I agreed to try an anti-anxiety medication again, namely Chlorprothixene. It was the very lowest dose I was given, and I started by taking one tablet in the evening. But it didn't go so well. I had a drop in blood pressure from the tablet, and I fell and hit my head on the bathroom threshold and got a long wound on the scalp. I probably bled a lot and even passed out for a while. Naturally, I should have called for an ambulance, but I didn't. No, instead, I pulled down a knitted cap, went out and scraped the ice off the car – it was apparently freezing, down to 20 degrees below zero – and drove myself out to the hospital. Once there, I was at once laid on a bed and sutured with eight or ten stitches. I probably also had a fracture of the sixth vertebral arch in the neck, but it was not something I found out at the time. That is what can happen when you are sensitive to medication. And stubborn.

✂ ✂ ✂

The psychologist and I stubbornly fought on, although I was always stressed and scared, and she must have been quite frustrated. As I said, I certainly had the feeling that we didn't fully understand each other. That there were things that I as a human being should know, do and understand, but like darn didn't. Unfortunately, something I don't think I could put into words and explain to my psychologist.

But I do know that over the years, I time and again said that it felt like having a big question mark inside, but like darn lacking the ability to formulate any real questions. That I was like one big yarn tangle, but where I could not even get hold of any end to start to sort it out. Unfortunately, some of this tangle I still have within me. However, I have now at least found several ends to separate and then slowly but surely also begun to understand myself better.

"It is a constant commute to and from in the contact, and the patient expresses both her longing and her great fear. She feels terrified when she does not know what is expected of her and she feels so failed when she thinks she is 'freaking out'." (Psychologist)

"Has now, after a period of increasing approach, withdrawn again and is more measured and uncommunicative in the contact. It then becomes rather quiet in the room, which is why it is difficult to have a dialogue." (Psychologist)

More hospitalizations and moving

Eventually, my suffering once again became almost completely overwhelming; my body was about to break, and mentally I felt even worse. I didn't have access to any knowledge that could help me understand my difficulties, find ways forward, or more easily endure the present. So the only thing I could hold on to was the psychologist and her beliefs – but also to the district doctor and my family, of course. So when I didn't understand what I was struggling with or for, I kept on fighting for the psychologist. Because if there was a person for whom I wanted to "succeed", it was for her. At least I wanted to be able to give her the gift of being a good patient and getting well when she fought so stubbornly and infernally for me.

Therefore, in the spring of 1999, I again agreed to be admitted to a hospital, this time to a regular psychiatric ward in Falköping. It certainly was not easy for me, that much I can say even though I don't remember it. I know, for example, that the situation with my mother was much more complicated than when I first was admitted to Skövde hospital, because this time she was much more in need of help. So I went out to see her as soon as I was on leave. But the actual stay in the ward was, of course, the worst for me, with all new contacts, all new and continuously changing impressions, all agony – both my own and others' – and all uncertainty and this nagging about medications.

"Finds it hard to be in the ward with so many people when she has difficulty with close contact. It is not the people themselves, but the actual contact with people she experiences as tough. Like choosing between plague and cholera according to herself." (Doctor)

The first time I apparently could not endure more than three days, but the psychologist persuaded me to try again and then I managed to stay almost two months before it all became overwhelming. But at least I had now met and made very good contact with a nurse in the ward – a person who was easy to talk to and who also came to mean a lot to me.

During the summer, I contacted the ward again regarding self-admission, even though it was on my psychologist's advice. This time I was in for as long as seven months. It was pretty brave of me; I can now think. Because I both see and understand that, for example, I must have felt awful just by not being able to specify what I actually wanted help with, in addition to a period of physical relief then. I find it very hard to understand how I managed to fight like this, year in and year out, when I didn't even know what I was struggling with.

But I did struggled, damn it. And I get sad when I see how I kept believing that *all* the painful feelings were a sign that I was going somewhere. That perhaps even I was becoming a "normal person". And therefore, I continued to put pressure on myself even the times I should have understood that these feelings were actually more of a warning sign I should have listened to. That if the inside screams "Run!" sometimes you should do just that. And then neither despise nor punish yourself for it, which I constantly did. The fact that I felt so terribly bad in contact with psychiatry, I also think should have made the alarm bells ring with them, made *them* understand that maybe it was something that they/we did wrong here.

"During the conversation, we try to discuss a little bit about what the patient wants to get out of her stay and what we should do. Malin does not know this for sure and finds it troublesome that she cannot really specify her wishes." (Doctor)

"She is having a tough time in the ward, and in many cases, it is far too difficult for her to be around people like that, and the fear often prevails, and she is close to the breaking point and also over the breaking point. Saves herself by going out for long walks or leaps and bounds and by being able to go home and be with herself in her flat." (Psychologist)

As I said, I had made good contact with a nurse, which was probably mainly what kept me in the ward. In addition to the psychologist's belief that it was good for me after all, then. Which it naturally was, at least physically speaking. But it was extremely exhausting and stressful to feel that the doctors wanted me to medicate and function in a certain way. And also feel that other staff members considered me difficult because I didn't make any progress and ran from the ward when I could not stand it. Here my diagnosis truly put me in the barrel. And many staff members probably saw me as manipulative, something I indeed am not, and as a person who overreacted over and over again.

"The patient is very tense, wound up and stressed but still manages to sit for a whole hour and talk to us. Does not make eye contact but still tries to talk about the different things we are discussing. Feels that she has to fulfil duties in all directions." (Chief Physician)

"The staff in the ward feel some frustration because they find it difficult to know what to do to help Malin. Think that she is not making any progress." (Chief Physician)

"She feels extremely failed that she cannot stand being in the care environment. At the same time, she has difficulty coping with being at home, and there is a lot of food on the leaves she has." (Psychologist)

I find it very difficult to understand that I endured this as long as I did, and I fully understand when I now see that I so often thought about discharging myself. But at the same time, I was continually trying to adapt to the situation. I constantly tried to adjust to what the near future would most likely look like, so I almost panicked every time something unexpected appeared. Something that the mental health service obviously didn't understand at all. Having to meet new caregivers, for example, is stressful for me today, so then it must have been awful to have to do that so often in the ward.

❡❡❡

In yet another attempt to both make me better understood and better understand myself, I asked at this time for a new meeting – this time with the nurse, the psychologist and the district doctor. I felt that I was not getting anywhere in the ward and hoped that such a meeting might make me a little wiser.

"Malin tries to make herself understood with us and is very careful to explain what is really completely impossible to say in words. She also wants to hear our answers and whether we say roughly the same. She still cannot trust that we will be with her no matter how she behaves and how she feels inside. She wants to do, say and think right, and she also wants to show the right feelings." (Psychologist)

But in any case, my psychologist thought I was making some progress during the care period. That I was more comfortable and less tense when I was with her, had less bond with my mother, and also was not beating myself so often and drank less. She also thought it was positive that I was trying to make more new contacts. And sure, that may be true in a way because, as I have already written, I work best if I get and have the opportunity to focus on one thing at a time. And in a way, I got the chance to do that during this period, even though the hospital stay was torture for me, and I, therefore, paid a very high price for it. What is also very sad is that it would have been possible to make the stay at least somewhat less painful for me, if only the knowledge that the doctors also gained had been applied much better. Namely, the one that I and the psychologist, through trial and error, had already come up with.

> "Malin's psychologist declares /... / Malin's need is to have quite a few people around her, and they should speak a clear language. Malin easily misinterprets when you are unclear. Needs structure in life. Also needs to feel that it is okay for her to leave the ward if she feels unwell. Important when it comes to Malin is also not to do too much at once, but to slowly move forward and all the time sees to what Malin wants and how she feels." (Chief Physician)

> "The patient does not make eye contact all the time but sits and looks down at her knees. However, she is very eloquent and describes her view of the care with which she is dissatisfied. Thinks that we strive in different directions, where the ward demands on how to be, and where the ward thinks that you feel good if you behave in a certain way, but that she herself inside feels bad." (Doctor)

Even though I felt so bad in the ward, it was still decided in January 2000 that I would stay for a while longer. Needless to say, I then tried to adapt to the decision and took it for granted that the hospital also should follow it. But that was not the case. No, instead, I was called shortly afterwards to a meeting with one of the doctors – a day when my contact person (the nurse) was not present – who made the decision just to discharge me all of a sudden.

The fact that he pulled the rug out from under my feet like that made me feel horrible. Especially since no one else in the ward even lifted a finger to prevent it. My psychologist was also wholly confused and enraged, and a deviation report about the incident was written. Now again, it became utterly chaotic in my head.

123

"Trying to sort out thoughts and feelings after what happened in the ward, but cannot get it together. The patient remains extremely distressed and copes only thanks to her extreme stubbornness and perseverance. She gets very hurt in her home with binge eating, alcohol and hitting herself. She has pain all over her body because she is extremely tense." (Psychologist)

After a month, a second treatment conference came to fruition, and it was decided that I would, after all, make a new attempt in the ward. Nothing that I neither wanted nor really could handle, so it was just barely that I managed to go back.

Of course, I don't remember this incident, but I am almost sure that it was then that my psychologist, when she saw that I was almost imploding with anxiety, pulled me down on the floor and squeezed me in her arms, half-lying over me. For someone who, like me, is not especially fond of hugs, it could have had the opposite effect, but here it calmed me down. She helped me understand that there was still an outer limit and showed that she saw and understood my terrible plight. I don't know whether we had already talked about Temple Grandin's hug machine or if we did it afterwards, only that at this time, we did at some point. In any case, in this way, I was helped to calm down and then dejectedly accepted the terrible situation. Once the doctor in charge of admission arrived, I was instead heartbroken about life in general and the hospitalization in particular.

"It is impossible to communicate with the patient. She does not answer questions. She looks at the floor and cries all the time. The patient is depressed, anxiety-charged. Do not want to talk or be examined." (Doctor)

I managed two or three months before I discharged myself and instead continued as a day patient a couple of days a week. In that way, I had the chance to meet my contact person and have access to a new, more healthy routine while at the same time having access to my routines at home. I had a couple of tufts to jump between to avoid being alone in the abyss: the psychologist and the nurse. But I can understand that I didn't want more, that I didn't want to become a regular day patient and go to therapy, for example, because both new contacts and the ward itself I had indeed had more than enough of. I obviously still had a little self-preservation, even though I was hurting myself at home at the same time.

❧❧❧

I know that during these years, my psychologist found an interview with Gunilla Brattberg, and after having now looked in Svenska Dagbladet's (a Swedish newspaper) archives, I understand that it must have been the one published there at the end of 1999. After reading it at the time, I began to think for the first time about the autism spectrum and became curious about Gunilla's books. I indeed recognized myself in so much of what was described there, and therefore searched wide-eyed further with other authors where I found more of the same. I know, for example, that I read Gunilla Gerland's "A Real Person" at the hospital, and I also know that I discussed it with my contact person. I found, years later, a notebook from the hospital period, full of quotes from, among other things, the book just mentioned.

I can imagine that it must have been an exhilarating and liberating feeling to recognize myself in so much finally. But of course, at the same time, there were also descriptions of things I didn't recognize – mainly different behaviours – so, unfortunately, I still didn't stick to these thoughts and fought for them as hard as I should have. However, it is even sadder that psychiatry didn't do it, when there was so much here that could have explained many of my difficulties.

"The patient's condition unchanged. Still severe psychological suffering. No clear progress. Still, she experiences a lot of anxiety, does not want her medications. The patient herself thinks a lot about her diagnosis." (Doctor)

I am very saddened to see that neither the psychologist nor the ward has made any notes in the medical record about my thoughts, in addition to the doctor's note above. Because I am convinced that this was a significant event for me, and that it would have made an infinite difference if I had received support and backing around it. And then also got properly explained to me that I don't have to function precisely as, for example, either of these two authors. Got explained that I should not have stared so blindly at the differences I found but should have instead tried to see the bigger picture.

Okay, that I may have to blame myself for not better standing up for my thoughts. But at the same time, I tried to trust that psychiatry, and especially my psychologist, possessed more knowledge than I did. Besides, I was probably so stressed and anxiety-ridden that I found it difficult to think quite clearly at all.

///

During the summer of 2000, I decided to move to Falköping. It had namely become unbearable to be in my flat in Skövde. And I became increasingly stressed about meeting the neighbours or risking running into old friends and colleagues in the city. I felt more anonymous and free in Falköping and probably hoped to get a fresh start to my life there. Besides, my caregivers had pointed out for so long that I was too caring and tied to my mother, so I wanted to show them that I could create some distance from her – literally.

In practice, the move certainly took its toll on me, both physically and mentally. But once I have decided on something or have clear plans and projects to implement, I also make sure that it is done. Stubborn and perseverant are my middle names.

> "The patient is not looking forward to moving to Falköping, but she still carries it all out because she has made up her mind. She also wants to show us caregivers that she can do it." (Psychologist)

The move itself I mainly carried out on my own as I usually want to fend for myself, although at the same time, it can get a little too much "can do it myself" sometimes. I drove shuttle traffic between Skövde and Falköping and moved everything that could be pushed into my and my mum's small car. Yes, I know my brother wondered what the heck they were going to move once he and my sister-in-law's father came with the truck. It was then only the largest and most unwieldy things left in my old flat. And as I hardly need to point out anymore, I have no recollection whatsoever of this move either.

When I finished moving at the end of October, I was wholly drained. Because even though the time before and during the move had taken up an extreme amount of both my time and energy, I had still had plans and a project to complete. Something that I could have stuck to and that has thus given me a certain structure and anchoring. Once this was done, I suddenly stood there with nothing at all. And I now also had to try to get used to both a new flat and a new city, although I already knew Falköping quite well.

"She experiences an intense emptiness and a very large alienation, and subjectively everything just feels worse now that she has moved." (Psychologist)

"Meets the patient this time in her new home in Falköping and, as I have now imagined it, she has arranged and decorated it absolutely incredibly nice and beautiful. The home represents the perfect shell that the patient is trying to show to her mother and brother, while I see the great contrast to the little frightened baby bird that sits and trembles at the kitchen table and does not know what to do." (Psychologist)

Unfortunately, this change was probably too large for me. A big black hole opened up in front of me, and I felt much worse than before, with increased anxiety and increased food and alcohol abuse. The move that was supposed to be the beginning of something new and hopefully better came instead to be for the worse for me; I lost my footing and probably fell pretty hard for some time. Here I really would have needed something to hold on to, such as a diagnosis that would have better described *the cause of* my difficulties. Something I could have seized and started exploring there in my solitude. And as in the extension also might have led to me being able to connect with people with similar difficulties.

I obviously could neither stand myself nor be alone in my flat. So in trying to get away from both, I stayed as much outdoors as possible on the days when I was not with my mother. I wandered up and down the streets, but I probably also spent a lot of time out in the forest. I understood that I had to build up somehow and get used to new routines, but that is easier said than done and can also take quite a long time.

In my super-stressed state, I now started drinking significantly more and then not only in connection with my food addiction. Yes, I even showed up drunk at my psychologist. Something I am very ashamed of now that I am sitting here reading about it. It was, of course, incredibly stupid of me. Still, at the same time, it just shows how horribly bad I felt and how stressed I was by neither understanding myself nor having access to a more understandable and reasonably predictable world.

"She cannot be alone with herself in the flat for a long time without drinking alcohol, binge eating or maybe dozing off during the night for a few moments. Otherwise, she is out walking hour after hour to keep away the strong impulses to kill herself that she has. What prevents her from doing this is the responsibility of the mother." (Psychologist)

"She is asking for help. At the same time, she is unable to be in an inpatient ward with the hypersensitivity and susceptibility she has to other people and the need to please everyone, and at the same time needing to be in control of everything that happens. It will be an impossible and unreasonable situation for her." (Psychologist)

"The patient's feeling of being different and standing outside everything is very intense, and her attachment to a survival pattern that is devastating is so

In the end, my psychologist did no longer accepted the situation. She felt that we were not getting anywhere in therapy and that it was, therefore, time for me to be admitted. After mustering all her powers of persuasion, she finally got me up to the detox clinic again for a conversation with the chief physician. But even though these two women were very stubbornly trying to change my mind, I still didn't agree to a new admission. However, I agreed to come back to the ward a few times to show that I could abstain from alcohol. And I also returned a few times to talk to the chief physician, with whom I had already made good contact.

✦✦✦

My psychologist probably became, quite understandably, increasingly frustrated and resigned about what our situation looked like, and it truly saddens me to see how hard it must have been for her. But the gods should know that it also hurts a lot to see how resigned, terrified and frustrated I was myself. And how I constantly fought like crazy in my attempts to do, think and feel right.

"She sometimes has contact with [the chief physician], but the patient does not feel so confident that she dares to admit herself, nor have there been conditions for or anything to win with LPT. However, it is clear that the patient suffers very badly both physically and mentally, and I do not know how this will end." (Psychologist)

"Several phone calls from the patient where she is usually deeply despairing, anxious, crying and screaming out her despair and distress. In the middle of this, she maintains her visit to the mother in Skövde. It is currently not possible to do any actual psychological work." (Psychologist)

"Expresses with great agony how unsuccessful she feels and that she is a burden to us, beats herself with her palm to her head, scratches her hair violently." (Psychologist)

She felt there needed to be more caregivers around me. At the beginning of the summer of 2001, therefore, she turned to outpatient care to try to establish contact with a psychiatric nurse for me. Something that made me extremely stressed, but I still put some hope in, not least for the psychologist's sake. But then having to go and wait for something that I didn't know how it would turn out, well, could not even imagine, was extremely difficult for me. So there were many crisis reactions in those months before the nurse's first meeting came about.

To go and wait, especially for something that is uncertain, is plague and torment for me. Therefore, I want to get things done as quickly as possible to have access to a more predictable future. Otherwise, there is a significant risk that the panic will instead become a fact, and I will ignore it all. Hence I can sometimes be a little strenuous to deal with in certain situations. The psychologist understood a lot of this, but yet I see that she usually, and so here too, described my problems in establishing and maintaining contacts often as feeling "disappointment and offence". Or feeling "rejected". Something that is not quite right.

∥∥∥

Now the psychologist's contact became increasingly uncertain, as she dismissed most of her patients and instead focused on other tasks. Thus our meeting times became a little more uncertain but, above all, more irregular, which was also very stressful for me.

> "It is difficult to know what to do in situations like this when the patient is getting upset whether she gets appointments or not at all. However, she is right that the care cannot at all give her what she needs in terms of continuity, security and predictability, in a way that she dares to relax so much that she can dare to land in herself." (Psychologist)

> "The patient is lean and frozen and 'stressed out'. Chasing around in life and with her eating, so as not to be forced to stop and feel the chaos and bottomless fear that still occasionally comes over her. The patient now suffers particularly greatly from the irregularity of our times." (Psychologist)

So far, I had also had some continued contact with the nurse I met while I was in the hospital, even though she had now retired. But sadly, our contact came to a less successful end, which was probably also my fault. I had presumably continued to be as honest as possible about my distress, which had previously been encouraged, and it goes without saying that it would be stressful in the long run for anybody out-side the healthcare service. I probably should have tried to play a much more pleasant and cheerful Malin in contact with her, I guess. Then I might not have driven her away. But now it turned out the way it did, namely as a new failure on the relationship front.

Thus, a lot stressed me and filled me with unanswered questions and anxiety now, but I was probably most afraid of meeting new caregivers again. In other words, I felt anything but fine once I got to see the chief physician and the psychiatric nurse at the outpatient clinic in late autumn.

> "What makes it particularly difficult right now is the patient's escalating fear of visiting the psychiatric clinic, and her ambivalence about this is very tangible." (Psychologist)

> "Meets the patient together with [a psychiatric nurse]. Malin describes her difficult situation, her strong anxiety and depression. Describes a ritualized pattern of living in which routines are a strategy for survival. We also talk about the patient's thoughts and wishes regarding the contact here, but Malin has a hard time expressing her needs." (Chief Physician)

In any case, it was decided that I would get a psychiatric nurse contact. And before the first meeting with the nurse, I was also tasked by the chief physician to try to formulate my thoughts about the contact and what wishes and needs I might have. Something I neither knew nor could manage myself, but had to turn to my psychologist for help with. So I came to the first meeting with a list compiled by both of us.

But unfortunately, I still didn't truly understand what to do there, what to talk to the nurse about. The only thing I soon understood was that I would clearly do something entirely different from what I did with my psychologist, and that the need I had to talk about similar things with them was wrong. I also didn't get any actual contact with her. Something that also stressed me a lot. I didn't dare to bring it up with her myself, but my psychologist also had to help me get closer meetings to perhaps more easily establish contact with the psychiatric nurse that felt good for me.

Although closer contacts initially made things a little easier for me, it still didn't feel good. But despite that, I struggled and hoped that it would still work out somehow, even though I mostly stuck to the contact for my psychologist's sake. She had namely wanted to have this done from the beginning to help establish other contacts for me as well. So she asked me to persevere even when I felt I had had enough a long time ago.

> "The patient expresses that she does not feel really understood by me, but has difficulty describing in what way. She says she comes mainly because [the psychologist] has said she needs further contact in psychiatry." (Psychiatric nurse)

> "The patient needs support and help in different ways. What I have been able to offer so far has been anxiety-creating for the patient, and both she and I feel that we do not get a good contact." (Psychiatric nurse)

Continued struggle in the same rut

I just felt worse and worse and was in a purely deplorable condition, both physically and mentally: "is extremely thin, has pain throughout her body and often walks limply and even crouched, is stressed out". I was also totally resigned to the whole situation. Something that, of course, the psychologist must also have been. She felt that I had such severe suffering that they had to try to build a much clearer support structure around me, especially since I could not cope with being admitted. So, in addition to having contact with the outpatient clinic, she put forward the idea of also contacting the municipality's psychiatric staff.

"The patient is currently very resigned to her and our possibilities to help her further, and she has pronounced suicidal thoughts and is now talking more about the plans she has had since long." (Psychologist)

"Continued inconsolable attempts to be of any benefit to the patient. She experiences herself, and so do I, that she ties herself even tighter and that she becomes more and more silent, ties herself together and falls into intense crying, which then continues. I believe that she has a clearly greater need for care than we can meet in outpatient care; at the same time, she is panicked about everything that is called inpatient care, and I have also seen that she gets very hurt in that environment because it becomes too stimulus-intensive for her." (Psychologist)

In the summer of 2002, it was time for another stressful meeting, this time together with my psychologist, the psychiatric nurse, the municipality's psychiatric coordinator and a nurse. Before every meeting like this, I am, as I said, more or less panicked, so I guess I was that this time too. Then I also got to meet the municipality's staff alone a couple of more times before it was decided that I would receive support from them in the form of a contact person. Something I didn't genuinely want to have but also was ashamed of, so here was added another stress element because I didn't want to tell my family.

This summer was also my second nibling born, this time a little boy. Naturally, it was an immense and happy event for my family and me, but one that I, unfortunately, have no memory of whatsoever. I am so incredibly sad to have to write these things – but even more sad about to actually have these terrible memory difficulties.

At the end of the summer, I started seeing the contact person. It went reasonably well, at least initially, but then it just became increasingly stressful and anxiety-filled for me. I have no memory whatsoever of this woman and don't know what we did together, although I can see that I let her into my flat. Probably we talked and walked a lot, I guess. But doing that with someone who does not understand me, I have nothing in common with, or at least shares an interest with, is not only meaningless but also painful for me. In any case, I know that I didn't feel good about it, and it is also apparent in my medical record that I only felt worse from the contact before I finally ended it in late autumn 2003. Another breakup for which I, of course, blamed myself; another failure.

///

By now, I had also ended my contact with the psychiatric nurse. But since the psychologist felt that I needed to hold on to the clinic, and I also felt that I probably needed someone to talk to in addition to her, she tried to get a new caregiver. Someone I could hopefully establish a better relationship with.

So now there was once again a lot of concern about what it would be like in the future. If I were to get a new contact at all and if it would work in that case, or if I would fail again instead. My panic and distress increased during this wait – but I also panicked when I finally got an offer. Therefore, I pressed the psychologist hard for her to decide how I should do, something she, of course, said I had to settle for myself. So for both her and my sake, I chose to accept, and in late autumn 2002, I started seeing a new psychiatric nurse.

In the midst of all this chaos and distress, I also became increasingly aware of and tormented by not seeming to have access to my memories in the way that most other people have. Hence I became increasingly intense in my search for answers to why I have such problems. Why my brain does not seem to function like most others. And I also continued to struggle more and more trying to understand, accept and manage my feelings.

> "The patient cries a lot during the visits here, almost incessantly, crying and snotting. At the same time, she becomes very stiff in her body and is in a lot of pain when she touches everything she finds so terribly difficult in life. Also now suffers a lot from the fact that she does not remember her own story, experiences everything so unreal and that she has no reference points." (Psychologist)

> "The patient desperately tries to keep full control of a situation, both in terms of the exterior and the interior, which is actually completely uncontrollable and which for her is very terrifying because it is so unpredictable. On and off, I think the patient uses our meetings here in a constructive way; either she is going through things that are relevant today or related to experiences from the past." (Psychologist)

> "She also thinks a lot about why she is the way she is and wants to try to understand in order to find some kind of security in her situation." (Psychologist)

January 2003, I also returned with renewed vigour to my thoughts on the autism spectrum. I now presented them to both the psychologist and the psychiatric nurse, with whom I thankfully came to have good contact, but certainly also with my district doctor. I was now thinking very intensively about how our brains and we humans really function, and read many books dealing with both neurology and psychology. Unfortunately, however, I also seem to have continued to listen to, or perhaps rather feel, the views of psychiatry. Thus I mainly searched for answers and understanding in books dealing with difficulties that may arise during childhood.

"During today's visit, the patient talks a lot about autism spectrum disorders, thinks she recognizes herself in many of those symptoms." (Psychiatric nurse)

"The patient also tries, by reading, to understand what has happened to her, and she finds different comparisons with people who have autism spectrum disorders, but also that there are significant differences between her and these people." (Psychiatric nurse)

"Otherwise, the patient has worked well during the period and has been very busy trying to understand how the brain works and how stress experiences and difficulties in managing emotions can cause wide-ranging disturbances in the ability to function. She puts what she learns in relation to herself, and thinks she gets something that helps her build something that can make sense. The patient returns to the fact that there are similarities between her functioning and that in people with autism spectrum disorder, but she still thinks that there seem to be notable differences." (Psychologist)

"The patient is intensely busy trying to find a common thread and context in her problems, which allows her to endure and move on with her life. She is very preoccupied with the fact that she cannot remember her story and that she cannot remember in a vivid way what is happening now continuously. We have recently compared how it works for people in general and how it seems to be for her, and I am becoming more and more aware that something essential is missing, which forms a basis for being able as a person to feel anchored in one's own self and see oneself in a meaningful context." (Psychologist)

I repeated time and again my enormous need to find out and to get help trying to understand why I function the way I do. And I actually think that by now, it was more than apparent, even for psychiatry, that there must be something more to the basis of it than "just" my up-bringing and my relationship with my mother.

After all, the medical record now contained so many and clear descriptions of my difficulties and what I might need. Besides, I had also presented both that and my history to many various healthcare providers: doctors in all forms, nurses, attendants, psychologists, counsellors and occupational therapists. Hence it is so sad that neither the psychologist nor anyone else began to think about any other cause of my difficulties. Understood that now it might be high time to look at them from a different perspective, especially since the psychologist herself had given me that article about Gunilla Brattberg at the end of 1999.

"Tired. Worn. Sees no future for herself. Feels that she is so different compared to the rest of us and this is getting harder and harder to put up with." (Psychiatric nurse)

"She tries to manage life by increasing her need for control, and it is then about binge eating and other forms of routines and control. At the same time, she tries to receive the thoughts and feelings that come around herself, how she feels now, her relationships on the family level, and also how she has had it in the past. She suffers greatly from not being able to remember practical details or events from her childhood, and she does not have a single memory of her father, for example." (Psychologist)

"The patient constantly apologizes for being a 'freak' and for behaving the way she does. She apologizes for her existence and for the person she is and the imprint she makes in the surroundings." (Psychologist)

✦ ✦ ✦

139

In the autumn of 2003, I made another attempt to put together things better and get clarity on what I was actually doing. I had already occasionally raised the question of a new meeting with the caregivers involved, and in the end, I also dared to ask for it in plain language. I can see that I now clearly said that I often felt misunderstood, but also myself had a hard time understanding, so I wanted to try to both reach out to the caregivers and at the same time become a little wiser myself. See if, in that way, I might be able to piece together all the different parts of myself that I laid out with them. The meeting went reasonably well, and I probably felt that the *caregivers* were striving in the same direction. And then, of course, I continued to strive with them.

"Our approach creates some kind of foundation for her, where she can feel a certain sense of security and dare to try to bring out what she actually stands for herself and not what is expected of her. The difficulty is that she is thrown in and out of different worlds and spaces all the time, and that most of the time she has to manage her life entirely on her own, with overwhelming anxiety and chaos for her." (Psychologist)

"The word horror constantly recurs in her relating, and it is especially noticeable when she calls that she is terrified and has a very high level of stress. Sometimes the fear and need for control take over, and she adds different compulsions, but sometimes she tries to remove, for example, opportunities for binge eating, not least to be able to achieve something in front of her caregivers." (Psychologist)

Sadly, in 2004, I put my thoughts on the autism spectrum aside again. Instead, I focused more on how badly I must have felt during my upbringing, and that I may therefore have used dissociation in trying to endure and deal with the outside world. The psychologist herself now often returns to this very word, and writes that also I am well aware that I blur painful situations and break up events. It is sad to see that I got so stuck in those mindsets, because then I must also have come to push myself even more in trying to bring about a change. Something that must have been counterproductive, to say the least. And indeed, I was just getting worse and worse. I also had constant and harrowing nightmares.

"Conversations about the misery the patient is in. Try on my part to encourage seeing or doing differently from that pattern. She still dissociates, and past experiences are also not available to her." (Psychologist)

"The patient continues to have severe suffering within her, between the different roles she thinks she has built up throughout her life, and that does not feel genuine to her and are not integrated into a whole. She puts an incredible amount of energy into trying to control an existence through different rituals and routines that she does not really feel in control of." (Psychologist)

"She has very difficult nightmares at night, and knows when she wakes up that she must have been fighting because she has often twisted her body in unnatural positions, and she has a lot of pain in her body. She has also had to acquire a night guard because she tends to bite inside her mouth. It is emotionally mostly about fear and being chased and put in impossible situations. However, she does not remember the content of what she dreams." (Psychologist)

♦♦♦

Now it is undeniably becoming very challenging to read my medical record, because it is so terribly painful to see that we just drove on and on in the same rut. Of course, I should have reacted more strongly to things I didn't think were right, but unfortunately, I had neither the knowledge nor the energy to do so. What is then much harder to understand is that no one in psychiatry reacted. Because I think it is now evident that it was not about emotional instability in me, but instead that I was constantly afraid and stressed about not understanding and not being understood, and therefore got meltdowns when it became too much for me. So, in a way, my and psychiatry's increased focus on dissociation was not entirely wrong, as I had to "switch off" painful and contradictory feelings and thoughts, and kind of put me on the outside of myself, to be able to continue with this inconsolable struggle at all. A struggle not only with myself and psychiatry but also concerning my surroundings and family. If I had sometimes not "switched off" or dissociated, I would most likely not have survived.

"As before, the patient struggles to try to keep away what she thinks and feels and what may be herself. Consider she is more stressed than ever, and it is also noticeable in her whole revelation how tense and strained she is, and she has also lost further weight and is very thin. She feels chased both by her immediate surroundings but also by herself." (Psychologist)

"The patient is tired, worn and thin. She is chased by her anxiety, her fear of what she carries inside her, which she does not really know what it is but who catches up with her. And by her endless chores, compulsions and rituals to maintain control and hold of all this. At the same time, she maintains her everyday life and service to her mother, and also tries to maintain some form of social surface towards the rest of the family. Sometimes something happens that breaks the routines and the mundane, and even more anxiety and feeling of being different and outside is created." (Psychologist)

"The patient works intensively at the psychological level to try to embrace what she feels and actually thinks for herself, and she is increasingly frustrated that she cannot within herself know and remember what her upbringing really looked like. She lacks almost completely concrete memories, and above all, she has no memories that have any emotional meaning whatsoever for her." (Psychologist)

Through trial and error, my psychologist and I had nevertheless come to many accurate conclusions, both in terms of what I would need and how I could handle certain things a little better. So when, at the end of the year, she suggested that we should try together to set up routines on how I might take on my everyday life, it was both right and good.

But at the same time, it must have felt – just as it does now when I read about it – both humiliating and like a failure, when in that way, as if she had given up, she tried to use my "squareness" to, in addition to routines, also make me understand that I could not control everything myself. If we had first understood why these routines were so important and necessary for me, I think we would have done better, but now we didn't. And then I probably just felt useless when I could not do things that others seem to be able to do without much effort. For me, it is important first to gain access to knowledge and understanding to then have a chance to find ways of accepting and dealing with difficulties.

So both this and the fact that I tried meant that I now felt even more useless and failed as a human being. Because yes, I was actually trying to make a change, albeit small, in one of my routines and then failed miserably. I know that when I got home from the psychologist, I tried, just in my mind, to replace a plate for tomorrow's breakfast and then became wholly panicked. Because I could not figure out for my life which one to take instead, and yet I had several of the same sorts in the cupboard. So I called the psychologist and screamed out my decision anxiety. It is admittedly possible to laugh about it today, but it was probably anything but funny at the time.

My self-loathing grew when I didn't even succeed in such a simple task. Yes, I blamed myself for the most part at this time, because all the failures must indicate that I didn't fight hard enough in trying to function "normally". Now I felt so distressed that again it was time to add some additional support, this time, an occupational therapist. And so the stress and anxiety of a new contact once again became a fact.

For a long time now, I had no idea what needs I really had, or at least didn't know if they could be considered "adequate", but I relied wholly on psychiatry. Sadly, this also meant that, above all, the contact with my mother had become increasingly stressful over the years. During these times, I was constantly torn between several different Malin, one of whom even tried to tell me that my mum and her illness were probably the main cause of my distress. It was tearing me to pieces then – and filling me with an immense sadness today, when my mum is no longer with me.

"We also talk about how it could have been like this, what possibly went wrong in her childhood. The patient constantly blames herself for being the one who has done wrong, feeling that she has no self of her own, but has always tried to understand what other people want, and then done so." (Psychiatric nurse)

"It is very strange that the patient still manages to maintain some kind of balance and can recover to the point where she does not completely collapse. As I see it, a safe care environment with a few people with good knowledge of this type of pervasive and severe psychological suffering could be beneficial to the patient, by being there in a more practical way for her, and partly preventing her from some of the compulsive problems but also ensuring that she can cope with what she feels." (Psychologist)

"Starts by notifying the patient that I have spoken to [the occupational therapist] /.../ The patient is afraid of not knowing what to say and that she has to present what she wants help with. She says: 'Help, I need to talk to [the psychologist] so she can tell me what I need help with', but we agree that we meet all three in 14 days and that she and I then help each other." (Psychiatric nurse)

EMDR and musings about the autism spectrum

The contact with the occupational therapist thankfully turned out well. Still, even in 2005, I put more and more focus on dissociation and now also on my diagnosis, emotionally unstable personality disorder. Because if psychiatry thought I was functioning like that, I too must find answers to my questions in this diagnosis – if I just searched properly and fought hard enough. But it certainly didn't make me feel any better. No, quite the opposite.

"The patient feels that she has a harder and harder time managing her life, how she pushes things away, puts them in different boxes, all so that the fear and anxiety do not become so unbearable. She does not think she will be able to live much longer, because she does not think her body will be able to cope with this. Talking about her childhood, and taking all the blame for her handling life the way she does." (Psychiatric nurse)

///

In April that year my father died, and it also made a mess of me both mentally and physically. First of all, I had (and have) no memory whatsoever of him, and it came to the fore at the time. It must have felt both frightening and sad to neither be able to remember nor mourn a parent, even if the parent had not been present and had not stood up for me. Then there were many hassles and inconveniences surrounding this death in general, including a will where it indeed became apparent how little my brother and I meant to him. So there was a lot of tension and anxiety within my family here, which stressed me and made me feel horrible.

In addition to the fact that my mother here felt mentally worse, she also became very seriously ill physically during the summer. Something that naturally also affected my well-being. And since she would now only become more and more poorly in the coming years, it also meant that I had to support and help her more in terms of, for example, contacts with the healthcare system and being driven to it.

❋❋

As the stubborn person I am, I continued to address how bad I felt about not having access to my memories. Since the focus was on dissociation – and that I probably could not manage to remember parts of my history – my psychologist helped me in the summer of 2005 to get in touch with a private EMDR therapist, to see if that form of therapy could help me. She also went with me to Gothenburg to see this psychologist, and that several times. It was something she absolutely didn't have to do, something that was not part of her work, so I was (and am), of course, very grateful that she chose to push the envelope anyway and supported me like this. Just like I am very grateful about all the rest she did for me over the years.

"She suffers a lot from not having her own story, but that everything she knows is constructed from facts that she has been told. She now wants to be able to meet herself and build something of her own, but there are too many obstacles for her to cope with this. However, she is looking intensively for ways to be able to move forward, which she believes is necessary if she is to have a chance of survival." (Psychologist)

"The patient suffers severely from having nothing of her own to be able to anchor herself in, no memory, either small or big. The patient feels physically and mentally very bad and feels that her strength is fading. She currently has severe nightmares at night and therefore sleeps very badly, worse than usual." (Psychologist)

From what I understand, these visits were initially *very* stressful and anxiety-inducing for me, although I have no recollection that this was the case. But it seemingly became more manageable over time as I then continued to see this psychologist. Unfortunately, the focus here also continued to be on my upbringing and that I must have been traumatized, so my thoughts about dissociation didn't diminish in the coming years; on the contrary. And I never got hold of any memories either, but this psychologist came to mean a lot to me despite that.

/ / /

I continued to struggle, but in 2006 I became increasingly stressed about not getting the slightest bit better, especially as I was now in contact with and took up so much time from several different caregivers: two psychologists, a psychiatric nurse, a district doctor and an occupational therapist. And the fact that my family also questioned and wondered what I was actually doing in psychiatry didn't make things any better. But of course, it was not just me who fought, but my caregivers also did their best to help and support me.

"Her anxiety and stress level are constantly at their peak. And the fear she has in relation to herself and to everything in the environment she cannot control and predict makes it difficult or impossible for her to function in a flexible way." (Psychologist)

"The patient feels pressure to bring about a change because she receives so much treatment resources." (Occupational therapist)

"The patient feels she is not making any progress, disparaging herself a lot around this." (Psychiatric nurse)

"Although we cannot see much progress, my opinion is that the contacts she has in healthcare overall are necessary for her. And although the fears in life are enormous, she has nevertheless achieved some security with us caregivers, where she can use us in different ways and address her themes with variations." (Psychologist)

In addition to being stressed continuously by putting all the time and commitments together and trying to feel better, I was also increasingly worried by feeling that the diagnosis that was put on me certainly didn't fit well. I had started spending a lot of time on an online site for people with the diagnosis of borderline, and I felt that I didn't truly fit in. Unfortunately, I was also almost burning out here, because I felt a great need to help and support and find it very difficult to defend myself when others feel bad. I was also frightened and saddened when I realized once again that psychiatry probably considered me to be a demanding and emotionally unstable person, something that some people on the site could actually be. It was a feeling that had previously been so tangible and painful for me when I was hospitalized the second time.

"Nothing new. It is clear that the patient is so stressed (jerks strongly at the slightest snap in the house) that she cannot filter either sound or more complex social messages. She thinks she has to come up with something, but cannot receive the instruction to take it a little beautifully and seek the recovery to be then able to take some new steps." (Psychologist)

"The patient is severely disabled in her personality disorder. With pronounced symptoms of anxiety, eating disorder (binge eating), forced rituals, where she pushes herself to the limits and follows structured daily patterns that go beyond the physical and mental forces she has and with alcohol abuse elements. The risk of the patient actively committing suicide is currently assessed as small, as she has a responsibility to her mother." (Psychologist)

"With some variation, it is all about her having to try to see everything as it is — she has great ingenuity in avoiding this. There is a great awareness that this is the case. Still, the horror, which she describes as unbearable as well as unknown, means that she cannot cope with it but chases on, plus she divides life into many parts, which work independently of each other and without contact with her own self. Loneliness, alienation and fear dominate." (Psychologist)

On this site, I also got in touch with a woman I was trying to befriend. We met two or three times and probably even had a lot of contact both on the site and via chat and SMS. But today, I don't remember either her or our communication. Sadly, this relationship eventually became too stressful for me, with all the constant misunderstandings and unsaid things I would obviously understand, but of course didn't. So I gave it all up. Another failed relationship, with subsequent self-loathing for not seeming to function like a "normal" human being.

However, thanks to this site and the contact with that woman, I became even more aware of how badly the borderline diagnosis suited me and my difficulties, which I raised again with the psychologist in

2007. It is so regrettable that she still chose to hold on to it, and here I can indeed be a little disappointed in her. I must have expressed how enormously hurt I was by it. And it had now also been clear for many years that with this diagnosis, I didn't proceed at all in terms of either understanding myself or finding ways to deal with many of my difficulties.

"She is also very tormented by not having memories of her life and that she still erases everything she is through, which means that no real inner frame of reference is being built today either, but she lives in a constant, terrifying readiness that anything can happen. Her approach to her own self is almost delusional, and she cannot help but feel the horror she feels about herself. It is to a very small extent possible to bring about change through psychological treatment and support. It is carved in stone." (Psychologist)

"The patient has great psychological suffering with significant compulsive rituals, including bulimia. She is very intensely struggling to find ways to manage her life while also fending off a lot. She has several healthcare contacts, where she works with her issues in different ways. Diagnostically, F60.3 Emotionally unstable personality disorder remains a collective designation, even if the patient notices in her online contacts that she is not like the other people there who live out quite dramatically." (Psychologist)

//

During 2008 and 2009, I continued to search very intensively for answers as to why I have, among other things, memory difficulties. And that from the point of view, I am probably dissociating and that I do so because of what I have experienced growing up. Now I also struggled with this with the private psychologist I went to Gothenburg to meet. I now read a lot of books on the subject but also books that addressed, for example, the theory of affiliation, and I fought hard to both understand myself and be able to bring about some change.

> "The patient has a lot of thoughts about dissociation, and she reads a lot about it. Thinks it is more massive in herself than seems to be the case in others. She is frightened about never being able to experience that she speaks from herself, but always from some part that she has learned to play. Gets terrified as soon as she approaches something that might be her own claim." (Psychologist)

As might be expected, there was also a continued focus on the fact that my routines and rituals were not good for me. And I then accused and despised myself for having to hold on to them anyway. Therefore, in my opinion, it is quite understandable that I had such a hard time "tolerating" myself and even was afraid of myself, as is so often described in the medical record that I was.

The food addiction was definitely not good for me, but besides that, I would have needed help and support in understanding both why it was so and that I actually require routines to manage life in the best way. I am convinced that I would also have found it easier to both accept and tolerate myself if I had gotten and understood that. *Now* I despise myself because I didn't understand or stood up for this better in contact with psychiatry, but at the same time, it was more their job to understand this than mine.

> "The patient suffers from compulsive acts and obsessive thoughts; this affects everything she does, everything from sleep to everyday activities." (Occupational therapist)

> "The patient continues to work on being able to manage herself, despite the emotional lack she has of perceiving herself as a person, and despite the painful

experience she has of not remembering her life. The care contacts she has are important to her, and she uses us all in her own way. However, it is difficult to see any major progress, and she blames herself for it. She has lately tried to at least in the morning take better care of her breakfast. When you hear the patient's reluctant concrete description of what she is trying to do, it becomes apparent what enormous difficulties she has." (Psychologist)

"Continued work on the problems the patient wants help with, but where it is very difficult to see that she is changing. She still thinks she gets a little something from time to time that helps her. She cannot experience with all her senses and not connect experience and feeling. Still, when she understands with her head and also encounters (in books among other things) descriptions she recognizes, she gets something and then also feels less outside." (Psychologist)

At the beginning of 2009, the nurse I had previously had contact with and who had come to mean a great deal to me passed away. I happened to see her obituary in a newspaper while I was waiting to see my occupational therapist. I felt very bad, but unfortunately not in the way I would have liked. I didn't feel sad because I could no longer remember the nurse. Something that probably made me very scared and maybe even made me think if I was not a pretty horrible person after all.

In the spring, my psychologist then told me that she would quit her job in a few months, which surely came as a bit of a shock to me, even though I had probably already understood that it might be quite imminent. I was now even more anxious and stressed about trying to make a difference, especially as I so desperately wanted to show her that I could get well. Yes, that was one of the biggest reasons why I had even managed to fight for as many years as I had done by now. Therefore, I came in the next few months to push myself a lot more to show at least *some* progress before she quit. I also raised the question again if it could not be that I function somewhat differently than most other people, purely physiologically.

> "The patient wonders if she still cannot have any biological fault that could make it impossible for her to experience what others do. She has stuck to the phrase 'out of sight, out of mind'. It is clear that she works very much that way even today. I cannot tell whether it is about inability or since childhood developed patterns, based on the need to survive and a tendency to isolate very strongly."
> (Psychologist)

This psychologist, who was indeed an absolutely fantastic therapist and human being, and who became one of the most important and essential people in my life, I don't remember today either in the way I would so much like to do. And that even though we fought together for over 13 years. Okay, it does not matter that I don't remember all the hard times, but I would love to remember all that was also good. What probably made me feel like I was important and worth fighting both for and with. And I would like, even more, to be able to remember if I could genuinely bring forth how much I valued her help and whether she could take it to her heart. Unfortunately, however, this damn memory does not allow me to do so.

Now I also became worried about my treatment, whether I would get the help and support I needed and what it would look like in that case. For example, I thought I didn't know my needs, or at least could not express them in the "right" way; there, I had instead relied a lot on my psychologist. But in any case, it was decided that I would continue to see the private psychologist in Gothenburg and my district doctor, in addition to the contact with the psychiatric nurse and occupational therapist.

The latter, of course, already knew how the psychologist, among others, viewed my difficulties. Still, it feels sad to see in the medical records that it was now stated even harder at their last joint meeting. Because there it says, they were "well aware of the depth and extent of the difficulties" I had. In other words, it was a continued focus on my personality disorder.

❦❦❦

So the inconsolable struggle in the search for answers continued. I went to the psychiatric clinic here at home, went to Skövde for talks with the district doctor, and went to Gothenburg to see the psychologist there. But not only was I increasingly worn out physically, but I felt really resigned and downright useless as both a human being and a patient. I could not bear to have it like this and probably had suicidal thoughts more or less constantly, although, at the same time, I did everything to keep them away from me.

"Describes how her nightmares severely torment her at night. Do not want to live like this anymore but get up and get on with her rituals. As usual, a lot of thoughts about how it could have been like this and that she should have known better when she was a child. And if she cannot remember one thing, it does not exist. And since she has not read about anyone else with the same problem, she cannot have it either." (Psychiatric nurse)

"Feels failed because she does not fight enough and gets the change she wants, that is, to understand why her memory function is as it is and possibly be able to remember things." (Psychiatric nurse)

But in 2010, thankfully, neurology and neuropsychiatry came up on the table again, when my psychologist raised the question of whether it might not still be some kind of autism or other neuropsychological condition. Then I evidently expressed very great relief, something I have no memory of. But the fact that she then continued to share these thoughts with me was also a relief and something I came to value very highly. Before that, she had also wondered whether my very vivid nightmares might not be some form of epilepsy, and therefore I had to undergo an EEG examination. Admittedly, I felt so bad from the flashing lights that the test almost had to be interrupted, but at least it was concluded that I didn't have epilepsy.

> "The patient is resigned and thinks she is not going anywhere in her attempts to understand why her memory function is not working. Says that if she were to stop fighting, life would be meaningless and if so, the alternative would be suicide. Has thoughts about autism, Asperger's and also her psychologist in Gothenburg has taken up this idea." (Psychiatric nurse)

When I now received support from a psychologist, this time, I didn't let go of the idea that it might be about some form of autism. And I now also became a member of an online site where I got in touch with people diagnosed with Asperger's syndrome, among other things. Finally, I began to recognize myself in so much, and at the same time, I gained a much greater understanding of how different our difficulties and ways of dealing with life can still look. Something I really would have needed to have access to many years earlier! Admittedly, I was still very resigned and tired of life, but then a light was still lit, albeit small. The psychologist contacted the psychiatric nurse, and eventually, the ball was finally got rolling. A referral was written for a neuropsychological evaluation, which then began in November 2010.

"Feels like it does not make much sense in fighting, that she constantly fails. At the same time as she can also think 'that if I do the assessment and then would get a diagnosis within the autism spectrum, maybe I could understand that some things I do may not be possible to change but just are so'." (Nurse)

Neuropsychological evaluation, somatic problems and Gillberg Neuropsychiatry Centre

Although I don't remember the neuropsychological evaluation anymore today, I am well aware that it was both *very* challenging and painful. Yes, I was more or less terrified even before it began, and became even more stressed yet also resigned once it started. For example, when I began by telling the neuropsychologist that I could recognize myself in the descriptions found in Gunilla Brattberg and Gunilla Gerland's books, he said that he didn't think that they had Asperger's syndrome at all. Something that probably made me both perplexed and resigned.

The tests were then carried out under unacceptable conditions, namely in a construction site environment. There was drilling and hammering; workers talked and clambered around in the corridor; the light disappeared a couple of times; the fire alarm went off, and so on. I was utterly stressed by all this, although I did my best in trying to ignore all the distractions. And I was stupid enough that I even blamed myself, and thought that I must surely be wholly useless and failed as a human being since I apparently was not even worth a reasonable evaluation.

"The patient is even more terrified before the start of the neuropsychological evaluation on Monday. Stumbles upon her words and says the wrong word sometimes." (Psychiatric nurse)

"Malin is coming for continued assessment. She has been concerned about the previous test session and possible misunderstandings. Malin has a compulsively pedantic approach to the entire evaluation. Filling in rating scales is carried out in great agony and accuracy." (Neuropsychologist)

"The focus of today's visit is the patient's dissatisfaction with the neuropsychological evaluation. She is highly critical of the fact that rating scales and memory tests have not been carried out in a suitable environment. The patient accuses herself of not being worthy of a proper evaluation. Wondering what she herself has done wrong not to being worth this." (Occupational therapist)

During the assessment, I became increasingly resigned and depressed. After all, this was the last straw I could try to grasp in my attempts to perhaps get an explanation for my difficulties, finally. And then it was carried out like this, as I think, badly and carelessly. How inconsolable I must have felt to fight so hard when at the same time, psychiatry didn't seem to be a willing participant at all. I had also hoped that the neuropsychologist would talk to my psychologist or psychiatric nurse, or at least read my medical record more carefully, but he did none of that. And when I asked him about the latter, he said that he had only read the last few years' notes written by my former psychologist. I think that is so bad that I don't even have words for it.

//

In April 2011, I was told that I had not gotten any diagnosis within the autism spectrum, and as a layperson, I could not say much about that. But I still had (and have) my opinions on some of the "evidence" presented and the comments about why it had to be so. As for the great difficulties of my autobiographical memory, I was told that it should instead indicate that it could not be any form of autism since, for example, those with Asperger's syndrome usually have an excellent memory. That may be the case, but I still find the comment somewhat illogical and don't think it is entirely correct either. Especially not after having encountered several people diagnosed with Asperger's who indeed have significant flaws in their autobiographical memory.

What I got instead was a new personality disorder diagnosis, because at least there were no signs that I would have a borderline personality disorder. Instead, I got one of "mixed type", where several traits were joined together in a single strange mix – including schizoid and autistic traits and social phobia. Nothing that made me the slightest bit wiser, and certainly not psychiatry either. For example, I objected directly to social phobia, but I didn't get any response. I also wanted to know what the neuropsychologist meant by schizoid traits and what they were in my case. Nevertheless, even though I, together with the psychiatric nurse and occupational therapist, later had a meeting with him, I never got an answer to that question.

"The patient is agitated and sad. Expresses a hopelessness and feeling of being worthless and not being believed. The risk of suicide increases with the patient's feelings of hopelessness." (Occupational therapist)

"During today's visit, the patient receives feedback on the neuropsychological evaluation that was carried out. The patient has difficulties reconciling with schizoid traits. She gets it pointed out that it is a small part of the assessment, that other elements should be more emphasized. And then especially that she suffers from bottomless anxiety, unstable self-image on the verge of extinction, and that this is seen as her primary emotional problems. No recommendation for further action can be given, and this is explained to the patient." (Occupational therapist)

Now I was absolutely resigned, because the "bottomless anxiety and unstable self-image" was mainly related to the fact that I didn't understand either myself or psychiatry, nor seemed to be able to make myself understood the slightest bit. I didn't know how to proceed at all – or if I would even be able to do it. And at the same time, I was given the task of giving it thoughts and presenting how I, together with my caregivers, would still do just that. How we would continue to work and what my needs looked like, and what the psychiatric clinic might do for me. Something I think was a little absurd since I had received a diagnosis that told me nothing, and had the need to work more based on the thoughts on the autism spectrum and my memory difficulties. In other words, things that there was no actual knowledge of at the clinic. No, then I would have had to turn to the habilitation instead. If I had been diagnosed with autism, that is.

As for my memory problems, the neuropsychologist didn't seem to take them very seriously either, but at least he recommended a CT scan to rule out organically conditioned causes. Something which was also absurd because naturally, it is impossible to see minor deviations on such a scan examination. But in any case, in November 2011, I got to meet a psychiatrist to see if I could get help with such a referral. It is a meeting I obviously no longer have any memory of. But I can still state that I must have felt awful about it, because I am both terrified and physically nauseous when I read the note in my medical record. I didn't receive a referral, but instead, I was told how wrong I was in my thoughts and how wrongly I took on my difficulties.

"During today's conversation, it emerges that the patient has a predetermined idea that she has difficulties thinking outside. She has very low self-esteem, a lack

159

of sense of identity. Today's conversation does not contradict the diagnosis of mixed, very early personality disorder. The patient appears to have an anaclitic depression, mixed anxiety problems with compulsiveness in her thinking, which in itself can bring the idea to autism spectrum disorder. The patient is negative-minded /... / I relate assessment calls and my opinion that the patient is not motivated for working on change. The patient has a strange body image and appears to have stayed in a regressed state. Thus, I estimate that the patient will not benefit from anything other than support at home." (Chief Physician)

So I had come across another person who neither seemed to listen to me nor to understand me. And neither even seemed to want to *try* to do so. It may seem that it must be nice not to remember it, but as I said, it still leaves a trace. Such meetings, or similar situations, are not only excruciating for me; they unfortunately also mean that something within me breaks down more and more. Something breaks, and there then seeps the energy and the will to fight on – both with life and with the search for the answers I so very much want to get hold of – slowly out.

/ / /

The psychiatric nurse advised me to talk to the head of clinic about how I had experienced the meeting with the chief physician. How steamrollered I had felt when, instead of discussing my memory problems, I had only received a lesson in how wrong I was in my thoughts about, among other things, the autism spectrum. So in February 2012, I did, and it was decided that I would see another psychiatrist, which I did in April.

I don't think that this doctor took my memory difficulties very seriously either. And since I had already done a CT scan in somatic healthcare, it was no longer even relevant with a referral. However, I was advised to try to contact a university hospital where memory research may be conducted, and was also told that I could try to get a special care referral for a second opinion regarding my autism spectrum concerns. But, as I said, the psychiatrist herself didn't seem very committed to any of it.

"During the conversation, which lasted for an hour, the patient is confronted with information that she has previously read medical record notes where there are some explanatory models about her symptoms. However, the patient does not recognize herself in the full description, and this is her opinion." (Doctor)

This focus on the fact that I had a personality disorder therefore persisted at the clinic. For example, when my contact with the occupational therapist ended in 2012, her final note states that I have "severe psychiatric problems with a diagnosis of mixed personality disorder". Another note from 2015, when I temporarily met her when I was about to have a new psychiatric nurse contact, states that "the patient has an extremely difficult problem as she has compulsive behaviour, among other things". In the autumn of 2015, I also got to see a new psychiatrist at the clinic. Still, she neither showed any genuine interest or understanding for my thoughts on the autism spectrum and memory difficulties. No, I had undergone a neuropsychological evaluation where my memory was tested, and it also was established that I have no form of autism but a personality disorder. And when I got to see another psychiatrist in early 2018, it was the same thing; she also continued to insist on sticking to the diagnosis of personality disorder.

And that is even though we discussed my contact with Gillberg Neuropsychiatry Centre and what we had found out there.

///

After the evaluation, I not only began to become increasingly resigned, but my somatic health also started its journey downwards. A journey I have unfortunately still not seen an end to. Naturally, I raised these new somatic problems with my district doctor, where they didn't fall on fertile ground. As I got worse and refused to accept that it was purely psychosomatic, she felt that she could not add anything more. That she could no longer be the care contact that she had been for 20 years for me. So our contact ended strangely, to say the least.

Needless to say, I was saddened, and both apologized for being a nuisance and thanked her for all the years we had met. Something I apparently didn't get much of a response to. This doctor had meant a lot to me, and I had undoubtedly always done my best in trying to show it as well, so this end clearly came as some kind of a shock to me. But today, I still have no real memory of either the incident or the doctor, just a vague knowledge.

The funny thing about this event as well is that the district doctor, the psychiatrist, and psychiatry in general, had been nagging me all these years about standing up for myself. Said that I needed to feel and express *my own* emotions, feelings and needs. But when I did just that, they instead, so many damn times, said or demonstrated that it was wrong of me to do so. That it is not the right attitude. That kind of discourse with a forked tongue can really make me get completely dizzy. Nor do I have any higher thoughts about people who speak that way, I must admit.

After this, I have had to change medical centres several times but still have not received any real help or support, although referrals have been sent, and I also got to meet various specialists. For, among other things, a significant problem remains: my medical record states that my symptoms are most likely psychosomatic, that I also have a personality disorder and that I am emotionally unstable. And with that text in your medical record, you, as a patient, have a minimal chance of being taken seriously in somatic healthcare. And especially if you like me, also have a hard time using body language and prosody to show how bad you feel. It is downright deplorable, but nevertheless true.

> "The patient describes a resignation over not being listened to and believed in. Both in terms of contact with psychiatry but also with somatic healthcare." (Psychiatric nurse)

> "The patient is sad and resigned that her diagnosis of personality disorder is from the medical record at the medical centre in Skövde, and that all doctors then read this and constantly interpret her symptoms as anxiety. Feeling powerless, do not know how to make anyone believe what she says." (Psychiatric nurse)

One way to get away from your medical record is to seek private healthcare. And this is how I managed to still receive some help; for example, I had neck surgery in 2014. A major operation that I should therefore have at least some memories of, but I don't. The operation went well, but I unfortunately continue to deteriorate and thus have had to continue seeking treatment for my somatic problems. Since it involves neck problems and various neurological symptoms, my struggle has mainly been about getting further, more thorough orthopaedic or neurologist examinations. And besides, to be believed at all. But it is something that is easier said than done, despite severe difficulties.

In March 2017, I even became so dizzy and weak that I collapsed and broke my neck, among other things. But even that didn't make the neurologist think it was worth examining me again. I then had to spend two weeks in the hospital, walk with a fixed neck collar for three months and get help from the home care service, but I don't have any real memory of that time either. However, I know that the situation felt very despairing at the time – to say the least. But suppose that one still wants to try to see something comical in this misery: In that case, it is possible to read in the medical record note from the emergency room, when I came in by ambulance, that I have a mixed-type personality disorder, emotional instability. Only then does it say that I have a wound in the back of my head, damaged teeth and nose and a broken neck. Ludicrously absurd.

The fight continued, while I became increasingly resigned. After more than two years of waiting for a meeting with an orthopaedic surgeon at Sahlgrenska (the university hospital in Gothenburg), I finally got an appointment at the beginning of 2018.

However, after a new MR scan, I was told in August that no surgery was needed. But the doctor took the symptoms seriously and therefore wrote a referral to the neurologist – but sadly, I cannot say that I was surprised when it was then again rejected. I thus had to seek private medical care again, this time at a neurology clinic, where it was immediately established that I have dystonia in my neck muscles. Botox and various medications were therefore inserted but unfortunately without any positive result. So my search for explanations for these symptoms and what possibly could be done to at least alleviate them – and now also the neurologist's search – thus continued. And when he felt that his own ideas had dried up, he instead wrote a referral to Akademiska in Uppsala (the university hospital), where I would be admitted in the future.

♦♦♦

Although, after the neuropsychological evaluation, I didn't receive the help and support from psychiatry that I had hoped for, I still had to get my act together somehow and fight on. I had to try to get a second opinion on my assessment. And thankfully, even my psychologist thought it was very justified. After some thought and some contacts, she finally contacted Christopher Gillberg, to hear if he had anything wise to say about my ailments and difficulties. And to my great surprise and joy, he offered to meet me.

In June 2013, we met for the first time, a meeting I don't remember, but in my medical record, the psychiatric nurse writes that I was very pleased with it. Six months later, I met him again and then also quickly met Nouchine Hadjikhani. They had both become interested in my memory problems. I apparently felt even better about that meeting, and since then, I have been in contact with Gillberg Neuropsychiatry Centre.

"Since the previous visit, the patient has been to Christopher Gillberg for further assessment. Will continue with memory examination after her herniated disk operation. The patient has received a lot of positive feedback from the meeting and describes how she felt a warm feeling in her stomach. I have never heard the patient describe this before." (Psychiatric nurse)

In recent years, I underwent several tests and examinations – including eye-tracking, MR scan of the brain, MEG and EEG – and have also had many fruitful conversations with several people there, and still have so. The contact with Nouchine, in particular, has indeed come to mean a lot to me. And then not only because of everything I have learned and still learn through it, but also because she always has both support and pep to offer me.

Through these studies and conversations, it has been established that I do indeed seem to have a reduced function in terms of autobiographical memory. But it has also been possible to see that I have, among other things, a hypersensitivity to mainly moving visual stimuli, and have also found other minor abnormalities in my brain. Christopher also said quite directly that I certainly don't have an emotionally unstable personality disorder, but rather an autism spectrum disorder. Something I was very relieved about – but at the same time sorry that it had to take so incredibly long to come to that conclusion. I finally took courage a few years later and asked if he might even be able to put it in print. And in the autumn of 2018, I received a certificate stating that my diagnoses should be autism and specific memory disorder, and not some personality disorder.

///

In recent years, I have thus had contact with people – in addition to Gillberg Neuropsychiatry Centre also privately via the internet – who have understood my difficulties better. And in that way, I have also gained a much greater understanding of these predicaments myself. Something that indeed has both been and is incredibly valuable to me! Finally, I have not only begun to understand myself and my difficulties but have also been able to increasingly accept them. I am therefore no longer as afraid of myself, which naturally facilitates something incredible in life. Not least in contact with other people.

But at the same time, I regrettably have to write that life on many levels has continued to be very difficult and painful. And that mainly because I have not been taken seriously in somatic healthcare. Because the worse I feel physically, the worse I feel mentally as well. For example, I don't have the energy to perform many of the routines I need in order to keep my stress and anxiety at bay. Besides, it is truly something of a mental torture to be treated in the way I so often am in contact with the healthcare, especially as I already have great difficulty in both asking for help and standing up for myself.

With increased knowledge and understanding of myself, another insight has also begun to grow stronger over the years, namely that of how significant the knowledge gaps in psychiatry have both been and sadly still are. And when you, as a patient, are at the same time in a kind of dependency position, that insight can unfortunately often lead to a mixture of grinding worry, fear and sadness. Yes, sometimes even to severe anxiety.

Personally, I have had a continued need for some support and help from psychiatry – in the form of conversational contact – both to have the opportunity to vent thoughts and reflections and create points of reference in my life. External points that, in addition to my own routines, not only simplify things for me but are absolutely necessary for me to handle life in the best way. So it would have both facilitated and been very nice for me if there had been a greater understanding of difficulties and needs similar to mine at the clinic. Instead, in recent years I have had to try to explain and stand up for the knowledge I now have, but like darn still need to read in the medical record that I have a personality disorder. And in this way, to never get to feel truly seen or understood – well, it is actually very painful. Especially since an inner voice at the same time continually points out that I should indeed be grateful to be allowed to come to the clinic at all.

So what has also begun to bother me more and more is this complex conflict inside. In terms of trying to deal with and balance the fact that most people have only wanted me well over the years, and that I should therefore not feel, for instance, the disappointment or frustration that can sometimes arise. And the great shame that *I myself* didn't understand my difficulties much earlier, and the needs and feelings associated with them, also torments me very much. Not to mention the memory difficulties themselves and the *very* great fear and sorrow they bring. And here I am thinking not only of the problems in obtaining memories of my past, because even having such a hard time creating "memories of the future" is, as I said, very anxiety-inducing and hard to handle.

"Has many thoughts about herself and how she is, function and why she did not understand things earlier in her life. That she might then have received better help, learned more in order to function better. One notices the patient's resignation in that she feels worse somatically and does not get any answers. Feels like it only talks about her unstable personality disorder." (Psychiatric nurse)

"The patient has a lot of thoughts about the fact that no one saw what she really was like when she looked for help in psychiatry, but took it for granted that she was the way she was because she had a mother with a mental illness. How she has always tried to please and do what they wanted, even if it has always gone wrong. A lot of thoughts about the borderline diagnosis that she received from [the psychologist]." (Psychiatric nurse)

⁄⁄⁄

So I feel like I now have a very great amount of mourning in front of me. Unfortunately, a task I have not had the opportunity to deal with properly yet, mainly because I have had to put so much energy into fighting in my attempts to be believed and to get some help in somatic healthcare. But also because I didn't get a diagnosis change in my psychiatric medical record until April 2019. Almost 28 years after I turned to psychiatry with my questions, and nine years after I myself more forcefully presented that it is probably just autism and memory problems at stake.

Undoubtedly, some disappointment, anger and frustration also need to find their way out, because there is certainly also some of that. And then I also need to try to find ways to put those feelings more where they belong, and not just turn them against myself, as I unfortunately still do so often today.

But the constant worry about everything I don't understand and the fear are probably still what bothers me the most. For example, I find it very hard to understand that things could turn out the way they did, and thus I have struggled in recent years to try to sort out some order in the whole thing. And I will not conceal that I am very afraid of the healthcare system – now both psychiatric and somatic. It is namely very frightening to know, for example, that the interpretation prerogative is almost always with them and not with the patient; that it is their interpretations that become the truth in the medical record. And this despite the fact that knowledge in healthcare has significant shortcomings.

Nevertheless, I still need some help in the future, some support to be able to continue to deal with all this fear, sadness and disappointment. But above all, access to a contact with whom I would sometimes have the opportunity to vent and think about the anxiety that so often arises due to my various difficulties, but who could also help me dealing with my memory impairment. A permanent contact that could both support me and help me create some structure in my life. But the question is whether I will get any such help in the future, and if so, where.

As I said, the psychiatric clinic has limited knowledge of autism and the mental distress that the struggle to try to fit into the surroundings can bring. Not to mention a lack of knowledge and understanding of the pain and various difficulties that memory problems similar to mine can lead to. Besides, after my autism diagnosis, I don't actually even belong in psychiatry anymore. No, I do belong in habilitation, which has more knowledge of what such a diagnosis means. But there, in turn – as I understand it – they don't have as much knowledge about mental illness. In any case, I consider this four-square division of patients, who most often need information and support on and in both of these areas, to be anything but optimal. Yes, the risk that patients will end up falling between two stools sooner or later is probably sky-high.

And just fallen between two stools, I have in a way done now – or perhaps somewhat *more between* the stools, as I have hardly sat on the right one at any time during all these years. Because after the diagnosis in April 2019, I was then referred to habilitation, where I had to come to a first assessment interview after a couple of months. However, no information about possible aid could be given to me at the time, but I would receive one later. So now I didn't know what would happen ahead, other than that I would at least be allowed to keep my conversational contact in psychiatry until the habilitation decided whether or not they could offer any help.

I don't ask for much support, so I actually think that it should be possible to get it somewhere – although I naturally would prefer to not have the need at all. But I didn't know if habilitation would be able to provide me with anything, or if maybe the psychiatry could change its view of patients with needs similar to mine – or if it would instead be the case that I would no longer receive any help at all. This has added further anxiety and fear to my already rather voluminous collection. But also sadness that this search for knowledge and support seems to have to continue, especially since my physical strength is on its way to running out.

It was only in January 2020 that I was allowed to come to habilitation for a second, extended assessment interview, this time with a psychologist, because my difficulties "appear to be complex". Obviously, I felt a great deal of concern about that meeting, both because of the uncertainty that each new encounter with a caregiver entails, and the risk to only being informed once the assessment was done that no help could be given. But despite my fears, I really tried to hold on to the hope, albeit so small, of still being offered some form of support. However, this didn't happen; but instead, I was told that contacts that are only supportive are not included in the habilitation's assignment. Or even any contact at all when you, like me, lack "actual problem description, goals or possible endpoint". So my goal to try to fight on with life despite my various difficulties was not a goal that seemed to have any value whatsoever. That habilitation cannot offer more permanent support is very bizarre, I think, because that, if anything, should undoubtedly be a part of their mission.

Besides the fact that they lack knowledge, a more prolonged support contact is not included in psychiatry's assignment either. Therefore neither there can any real help be offered to me, although as I said, I have still been allowed to keep my conversational contact so far. But what will happen ahead, I don't know, and that scares me. And it is not only that but a rather mixed bag of several bothersome feelings that go around inside me. Feelings that can also be quite contradictory: Shame on even needing some form of support – but at the same time a longing for someone who can see and understand my difficulties. Sadness, disappointment and frustration for not finding this someone – and at the same time continually having a bad conscience, feeling ungrateful and only a nuisance when I still (so far) have access to a conversational contact. And, of course, the grief of being who I am, of having the difficulties I have – but at the same time, I can sometimes even despise myself for them.

///

Even though I write here that I mourn, I don't remember all these years in psychiatry, and that even though I was hospitalized several times. Therefore, the grief I feel is perhaps more from a third-person perspective, even if it is nonetheless intensely strong. But some other emotional memories have at least been created, as much of what took place during these years was traumatic for me. So I feel horrible about many situations and tones that have something to do with psychiatry and its opinions, or that in some way remind me of it. Besides, I often place a huge part of the blame on myself, because the feeling of being a failure and not being right, even *being wrong* (as a human), sadly still sits very deeply rooted in me. And harrowing nightmares about all this, as I said, I also struggle with sometimes.

///

Another great grief arose in April 2018, when my mother died suddenly. An event that has also brought with it some nightmares. I have accused myself of not having better control of the healthcare and that not enough attention was being paid to her various symptoms. Considering my mother's medical history, I should have understood that she had pulmonary embolism and thus needed better care. But I am afraid I didn't.

Two or three weeks earlier, she had fallen in her flat and hit her head so severely that there was a bleeding (a hematoma) within her skull. I had to call an ambulance, and she remained in the hospital for ten days before being transferred to short-term accommodation for further rehabilitation. I myself visited her pretty much every day because I didn't want her to feel alone. I also thought intensely about what it would be like when she got back home, such as how much help she would need besides me, and how it would go.

The hospital had naturally discontinued her blood-thinning medication – which she was on precisely because of previous pulmonary embolism's – so that the bleeding would not worsen. Therefore, I should have kept this in mind when she deteriorated. Because she did steadily declined. She thus had to go back to the hospital, where they found that the hematoma had been refilled again. But also that she had an elevated CRP, and that a transfer to another hospital for surgery could therefore not be done before it was lowered.

Now both my brother and I began to be very worried about her, and also frustrated with both the treatment of our mother and the lack of information to us. Mum just got worse and worse, but nothing happened. In the end, however, we got to see a doctor who more firmly took hand of the situation and established that mum had a widespread pulmonary embolism. And that the healthcare had not kept an eye on her lungs. This was something that then made my brother and me report the medical care to The Patient Advisory Committee and IVO (who are handling complaints regarding health care), who also blamed the hospital.

Mum was now so ill that she had to be transferred to ICU, and my brother and I were watching her by her side. Due to circulatory failure, internal organs were knocked out, and the day after the move, her heart finally could not fight anymore. She died with the whole family gathered around her as my sister-in-law had also come in with my two niblings.

After this, I was filled not only with grief over my mother's death, but also with grief and fear that I would now probably begin to forget her and the last time we had together. And quite rightly, this is what happened. I no longer remember what I write here, and that despite the fact that all this time was very emotional, to say the least.

Just a week after my mother's death, I myself was sent to the emergency room for examination, to rule out that I also was walking around with pulmonary embolism. I had to lie in the same place as my mother had done at the second admission, and on my way to the CT scan, I even had to walk past both ISCU and ICU, where my mother had also been lying. But my memory had already begun to fade; at least, I could no longer imagine what it had been like.

When I passed ICU on my way home after the examination, I stopped and cried outside the door. Both because of the grief over my mother, and because I could not for my life imagine the scene that took place inside the door just a week earlier. Of course, it had been terribly painful and sad, but also so nice when we were all gathered to say goodbye to mum. It is thus an event I would so much like to be able to carry with me as an autobiographical memory. But I cannot. Instead, I now have to fight tooth and nail to hold on to this story. A story I have not only written down in several places but also retold several times. All to be able to hold on to it truly. Because stories are all I have, and if I don't retell them, they also fade. Then it is no wonder I "dwell" on certain things, is it?

My mother's death has also meant that my anxiety and fear have now increased again. Partly because of broken routines and partly because the opportunity to ask her about various things has been taken away from me. I no longer have anyone to turn to in order to get memories of my upbringing and family history updated, although my brother naturally has some answers. But most frightening and sad is the fact that I can no longer remember her properly. To not be able to imagine her and our life together. It gives a feeling I cannot describe in words. But it is downright ghastly!

///

This became a long and wordy chapter about my life and my contact with psychiatry, which I managed to describe mainly because I have access to my medical record. A record with seemingly very detailed descriptions of how I have felt and what I have been through, both in healthcare and at home. But in addition to that, I thankfully also have access to some of my own notes – both on paper and online – from which I have been able to get help.

Had I had to rely on my memory, all this could instead be summarized in just a few lines. Because I actually don't have access to any real autobiographical memories – in fact none, if we ignore diffuse nightmares and fragmented flashbacks – which can be brought to life within me. I only carry with me a very meagre and diffuse knowledge of what my life has been like *on the whole*: What I have been through; what I have been doing; what I have likely felt in certain situations; and a knowledge of at least some of all the people I have met.

Just as I wrote earlier, my whole life truly balances on a few fact pillars placed a little here and there. And trying to get by with their help alone can thus often be like balancing on a slackline, something that can be extremely energy-consuming and very stressful. Yes, sometimes so painful that the energy almost runs out.

Or to describe it with a poem by Åsa Jinder:

"The edge I balance on is sharp and narrow. It is impossible to calculate the length of the steps versus the risk of losing balance. Almost wish I could fall."

Part III

8

Managing life without autobiographical memory

"I've a grand memory for forgetting."

Robert Louis Stevenson

By using the previous examples of why our memory is so important to us, I will now try to describe how my memory difficulties affect me, as I at least believe, in my everyday life.

Firstly, memories help us both in the present and to be able to form an idea of the future. As I have already written, I have a tough time imagining the future. Yes, it is hard to imagine anything at all. (But here my aphantasia[2] also comes into play.) When I stop and try to approach even the thought of it, it feels like a big, black hole; an abyss opens up in front of my feet. Even an ordinary, more light-hearted conversation about the future – without consciously trying to paint a clearer picture – can actually cause me anxiety. Therefore, it is not so strange that I have felt extra bad when, over the years, I also felt the frustration of psychiatry over my difficulties in looking ahead and my lack of future plans, is it?

---

2. See more information about the condition in "A few closing words".

Because this black hole is so terribly scary and anxiety-inducing, I try to avoid it in different ways. Then, among other things, routines are excellent to stick to, both as a distraction and as something that can lead me forward at least a bit along the way. And that even though many times they can also make me feel so stuck.

Routines and habits are, as we have previously established, implicit memories, which we rub in by making them over and over again. And once they are learned, they are often immovable like a mountain and difficult to change. Everything new we learn is first filtered through the experiences we already have access to, and what is too unknown is thus often sifted away. This, in turn, means that changes in routines and habits can be difficult to achieve, at least if the changes are too significant. We simply like to stick to what we are used to and what we feel safe with, which is naturally also the case for me.

The routines also mean that I still have a kind of autobiographical memory to hold on to, albeit so short, dull and meagre. I have access to knowledge of what I did last week and know what I will most likely do next week. If I look up and try to look further ahead (or back) than that, I most often hit obstacles in the form of fear and severe anxiety.

As I have already written, I have been told, mainly by psychiatry over the years, that I have too great a need for control and am far too routine-bound. That I am almost compulsive and that it is not good for me, but that I would both feel better and have a more tolerable life if I could just find some way to try to break many of these routines.

As for the habits and routines that have been directly unhealthy for me, these opinions have naturally been entirely correct. And in addition to that, *I* have actually had, and to some extent still have, a desire to be able to break many of my other routines as well. A desire to be able to be more flexible and function more like the "normal" person I would often like to be. But although these opinions and pieces of advice have most often been given in all good faith, they have unfortunately often come to hurt worse, because I have felt so incredibly unsuccessful and worthless when I have failed to bring about a change.

After trying to break some of my routines, I can only state that it does not automatically translate into getting a more tolerable life. No, this rather leaves me standing straight up and down struggling with anxiety, because I often don't know either what to do or where to go. As I wrote earlier, new experiences are compared with those we already carry with us, and that what we recognize or at least understand we take in more easily, which means that it can be challenging to change habits. If you, like me, lack so many memories of previous experiences, it can probably lead to it becoming even harder to break already established routines. To me, it feels that way anyway. Because just trying something new that I cannot imagine, or at least find it very difficult to do, is not so "just".

/ / /

The fact that I don't *remember* so many of the things I have done before can lead to me experiencing a great deal of anxiety and stress even when I have to do something that I actually *know* I have done before, because it may feel like I am doing it again for the very first time. So although I often feel both failed and cowardly, I still usually stick to the routines I now have.

When I have done something *several* times before, it becomes easier because then I hopefully have managed to create not only an implicit memory, but also to put it into words and thus created for myself at least a "semantic episodic" memory. But the anxiety and stress are something I still have to deal with in most situations, because life in general and people in particular are unfortunately often quite unpredictable.

Therefore, when I am going to do something for the first time, or *as if*, I usually even then try to stay one step ahead of myself. I usually go on a reconnaissance trip – literally or mentally – and this way, I try to sketch out intellectually how the whole thing is likely to play out. But I also fill in what several other *possible* scenarios might look like, to hopefully conclude how I should behave best and what I should do to be able to deal with the situation when it comes. This applies to all situations, large and small, and I can at least give a couple of examples that now come to my mind.

For instance, if I am going to a meeting in a room or in a place where I have not been before, I often go there a few days earlier – possibly with the help of a paper map – to see in peace and quiet what it looks like and how to best get there. In this way, my stress will be at least slightly lower when the meeting starts because I will then recognize the place. And I have, for example, flown a few times, but still have no memory whatsoever of having done so. Hence I don't know how it all goes, nor what an airport or an aeroplane look like. If I were to go out and travel tomorrow, I would therefore probably be in an almost panicked state of stress – if I had not at least investigated the situation by, for example, searching for information and films online.

There is a sentence in one of Barbara Voors' books that really describes my attitude and how I try to handle situations like this that is clear as a bell-ringing:

"Do not like unexpected situations so I solve them in advance."

✧✧✧

Another situation where my lack of autobiographical memory is an albatross around my neck is when I have to leave a medical history. Because the doctors want to know how I have felt before – when the problems started and how they have since developed, etcetera – when I seek care for any ailment. To then answer that I don't have the faintest idea is not good for either the doctor or myself.

To make it easier for myself, I now read my medical records, because then I have at least access to several of the information I probably need to provide. However, there is still usually a considerable problem left, namely, to explain how I have felt in the past. After all, I can only feel how I feel here and now. And I can therefore often find it difficult not only to remember what it has been like before – although at least I have the knowledge that I then really felt much better – but also to make myself a perception of what it would be like to feel good.

✦✦✦

The autobiographical memory should also help us visualize who we are and how we fit into our surroundings. And also to create the feeling of an "I". I wrote earlier that I often feel like a leaf in the wind, which is how it is. Because I actually find it hard to feel how I really fit into the world. Okay, that I have and have had my given place in my family, and mainly as the daughter who has tried to support and help her mother, but beyond that? Who am I, what am I doing here, and where am I going? If I stop and think about it, which I prefer to avoid, I suffer from such a great sense of unreality. Yes, it is almost staggering. Not to mention scary.

If I cannot remember living for 55 years, have I really done it? And if I cannot imagine myself in the future, am I heading for it – and if so, what does it look like? Yes, the fact that my memory, or rather knowledge, is so terribly diffuse and meagre actually brings with it that I often wonder if the life story I am clinging to is true at all.

The fact that I am, as it were, in a constant "now" also means that I have some difficulties with the perception of time, which for example, leads to me not genuinely feeling and understanding that I am ageing. Of course, the fact that I have access to information – other people's stories, photographs, various documents and notes – means that I intellectually understand that I have both lived and that I am getting older.

But there is still something missing, and I suppose that something is the resonance in my body. And I don't mean the one that tells me that I am getting stiffer and frailer. Therefore, I have a tough time determining my age, and it actually gives a very unpleasant feeling of unreality and emptiness. Sadly, a feeling that does not seem to be easy to modify the slightest, even though I struggle to try to remember both what I experience now and what I have experienced before.

I continuously repeat things I have found out through other people's stories or have seen in, for example, various documents, notes and photographs. And then I go back to this information when I feel that my (semantic) memory is starting to fail. I also try to gather various facts in general regarding what the past has looked like on the whole, and the same applies to the present, to be able to build credible scenarios over my life, and here is both big and small important. Something that can help me is, for example, all the books I have ploughed and am ploughing through. But films can also be beneficial, and so can people's spoken stories.

When I am sometimes faced with questions I don't have answers to, or end up in situations that make me understand that I don't, I immediately start looking for the answers. And when or if I find these, they are then placed in my fact bank, where I hopefully have access to them when, for example, I end up in similar situations again. In this context, I have noticed that it is much more effective to read or think aloud whenever I truly want to memorize something. So to not only put words on things but to actually let them pass over my lips seems to be important to me. I suppose it is not so strange then that I often talk to myself?

///

When it comes to making an image of other people for myself, and even more so to have a functional interaction with them, my memory's shortcomings are not the biggest problem. But those difficulties don't exactly make things easier for me either. No – on the contrary. I can often feel both a little scared and stressed in meetings with others as I know that it is expected of me to share my experiences and memories sooner or later. And this is especially true in closer relationships. I am not afraid of *people*, but rather of myself and the difficulties I have. This constant tension and the painful feelings of not remembering can make me quite withdrawn, or at least can be perceived as quite distant.

Otherwise, I can probably at least outwardly seem to have relatively easy for me in contact with others. But it is perhaps mainly because I have so many well-rehearsed scripts – for how I should behave and what I should say, etcetera – to stick to in different situations. Yes, many of them are probably not even just semantic memories anymore, which I need to pick out more actively, but have, in fact, even become well-established habits. Thus become implicit memories that have more settled in my body. Therefore, in many situations, I can have access to that gut feeling that can lead me right, or at least right enough that I don't put my foot in my mouth too much.

Even the fact that I am very interested in people and what they have to say – yes, I am actually a pretty good listener, who also tries to memorize what others share – probably means that I can be quite easy to deal with. Yes, maybe even to like. I can sometimes get that feeling anyway.

Something that also makes it easier for me in meetings is that other people often take for granted that others function in a similar way as they themselves do. Therefore, it is usually enough that I don't make any drastic mistakes. Besides, most people actually seem to enjoy talking about themselves and leading the conversation in general, so in many situations, I can just be quiet, nod in agreement, or at least not disagree.

Often, I can also use the information revealed in the conversation and thus gain access to a topic I myself can spin further on. But even then my memory problems and my concern about going untruthful can cause problems. Because when I spin on and maybe even give in to trying to share some of my own memories, I can become so terribly unsure whether this ever actually happened. Unfortunately, it may mean that I sometimes express myself vaguely and uncertainly during conversations, but perhaps even more vaguely or even slightly changed the next time we meet. And then the other person can probably wonder what I am doing and if I am telling the truth at all.

What I otherwise have mainly learned during my life, and also became quite good at, is helping other people. So when something like that is needed and gratefully received, it can flow quite well in contact with others, even if the risk of then being exploited is undoubtedly also there. It is mainly when it comes to trying to meet others on more equal terms, when it comes to a more active exchange of experiences, opinions, feelings, etcetera, that it can, and it often does, go completely wrong. Yes, I have really failed a few times miserably over the years. There I simply don't have really good routines and manuals to follow, but I am probably expected to go by my feelings instead. Something I often seem to have a hard time doing.

As I said, I really don't think that my memory difficulties are the main issue here, but together with my other problems, they can probably actually still have some part also in my failures on the friend front.

***

Our autobiographical memory could also be of support and help to us in the downturns of life, but as I have already written, it does not seem to work well for me. Sadly, I have difficulties in really *remembering* people who have meant and mean a lot to me, and the same applies to former positive experiences. In other words, things that might otherwise be able to cheer me up in difficult times.

Instead, something that has been and still is very positive for me, that I can often hold on to when life is hard, is my love of books. They have indeed helped me in many ways over the years. Because in addition to comforting and entertaining me, they have also taught (and teach) me how many things work, but also how we humans seem to do it in many different situations. They have also been very helpful when it comes to getting to know myself, by both teaching me to better understand what I probably feel and putting into words many of those feelings. But unfortunately, my memory here too puts a bit of a spanner in the works for me, because I cannot, for example, imagine what various characters in books look like, or how landscapes and buildings do it, etcetera.

Not having access to your autobiographical memory is, as seen, not much fun. No, it is certainly not something I wish anyone else to experience and would, of course, also like to avoid having to deal with myself. But even though both the horror and the shame are enormous, perhaps the sadness is not as great as it could and should be, because I don't really know what it feels like to have a well-functioning memory. Surely what you once had and then lost should be missing and mourned even more, I imagine, because then you have something to compare with?

But although my grief may be largely more intellectual, I still grieve, because I would really like to have access to an autobiographical memory. Because not only is it scary, shameful and sad to lack it, but it also creates such loneliness. Just imagine finding it hard to interact with other people, and then add to that not even having proper access to oneself, in a sense feeling almost like a stranger to oneself – is not that the most tremendous loneliness of all?

In one of her books, Nicole Krauss describes a man, Samson, who has lost his autobiographical memory due to a brain tumour, but who, despite his loss, first sees it as a kind of freedom, an opportunity to redefine himself and his entire existence. But then he gets the chance to participate in a medical experiment that might give him the memory back, and gets imprinted with a very strong autobiographical memory experienced by another man:

> "He could hear Donald saying something else but it didn't matter anymore what, because then and there it occurred to him that maybe the emptiness he'd been living with all this time hadn't really been emptiness at all, but loneliness gone unrecognized. How can a mind know how alone it is until it brushes up against some other mind? A single mark had been made, another person's memory imposed onto his mind, and now the magnitude of his own loss was impossible for Samson to ignore. It was breathtaking. He sank to his knees.
>
> 'Sammy? I said, are you there?'
>
> It was as if a match had been struck, throwing light on just how dark it was."

9

What could my memory difficulties possibly be due to?

"One of the strangest aspects of living with certain kinds of memory loss is knowing that the forgetting is happening."

Floyd Skloot

Now we have tried to sort out and understand what an autobiographical memory actually is, and also what it means to lack one, or at least huge parts of it. But what could this be due to? What various causes could possibly be behind my significant memory difficulties?

When I was first admitted in psychiatry in the early 1990s, as I have already written, the focus was entirely on my upbringing and the difficulties we had in the family due to my mother's illness, but also on my relationship with her. I must have been both traumatized and too caring and tied to her, and so this was also the basis for my difficulties in contact with other people and then mainly with peers.

What I thus needed to do was to start focusing more on myself and my own needs, and get better contact with both my feelings and other people. Psychiatry simply felt that I needed to acknowledge and accept that I actually had my own intense feelings. And also try to lower my guard and start trusting other people, but at the same time, not be too naive and therefore as easy to exploit as I could be. Well, thank you, the golden mean is probably good, but oh so hard to both find and get around. At least for me.

As I already wrote, this way of dealing with my difficulties didn't go particularly well. No, it made me feel even worse instead. But naturally, one cannot deny the fact that it was crucial for me to both start trying to get to know myself better, and to understand and accept that our feelings are actually of the utmost importance to us. Due to the psychiatry's – and my own – lack of knowledge about my primary difficulties, however, it took many years before I could really take it to heart and start working with it in a more constructive way.

✓✓✓

As far as my feelings are concerned, I have probably tried, and to some extent still do sometimes, to put a lid on many of them. But then I am mainly talking about the strong ones, because it actually seems that I have some difficulties when it comes to reading the weaker. My emotions often seem to need time to grow before I even notice them, and even then, I can sometimes find it hard to put my actual feelings into words. Maybe this is another reason why I seem to react more forcefully than necessary in some situations?

This thing with feelings is a bit funny, because if I now have a hard time reading my own, I am all the more sensitive when it comes to emotions and moods in other people. Yes, I can be like the worst satellite dish, which just cannot help but catch everything around me.

Something that can actually be very stressful. I can instantly feel when something is not right, can feel those "negative" emotions such as fear, anger, irritation, sadness, etcetera. But of course, I can also find it very difficult to know for sure *what* emotion it is really about – and then I have even more difficulty grasping *why* the emotion or mood is now there. Therefore, I can sometimes wonder whether it may not be the case that *I* am contributing to or even causing the mood. In any case, I almost always feel that it is at least my job to try to bring about a positive change in some way. It may sound a bit arrogant to think that it is my responsibility to make sure that my surroundings feel good, but unfortunately, that is often how I feel.

But when it comes to my own feelings, I have certainly tried to control them once they have become strong – as when my mother was ill, in contact with psychiatry, or in other stressful situations – because I would not have been able to do as much as I actually did if I had sometimes not "switched off" so many of my own feelings. Because we are not exactly well-functioning when, for example, we are completely terrified and stressed out, or curl up in a corner and feel sorry for ourselves.

But I have already established and also tried to describe that I still experienced very many and strong feelings during all those years. And to this day, I carry many of them with me in my body. Since it was so scary and painful, it might be easy to believe that my difficulties in remembering are simply due to the fact that I have repressed much of what I have been through. But I don't think it is that "easy" because then it should be more about me forgetting *certain* events or episodes in my life, and not like now that my difficulties include my whole life.

✹✹✹

I wrote earlier that I noticed a difference in my "memories" from before and after the age of twelve, and I have thought about what this dividing line could be due to. If, for example, I may have been affected extra (emotionally) strongly by the various events that took place at the age of eleven or twelve, such as my grandmother's death, my parent's divorce and the move to another place. Or if it may be more about my brain's development, which is gaining extra momentum at this age, and perhaps even about hormones.

Personally, I think it is probably a combination of all that. I think the divorce, the move to another place, the new way to spend time with children and young people there – more like teens, unlike what it had been like before when we had instead played, built huts and vehicles, or investigated and experimented – and later, my mother's illness, meant that it now became essential for me to start thinking and trying to understand so much more than I had to do before.

This fact that we all, at that age, are starting to stand more and more on our own two feet also means that we can no longer rely as much on, for example, our family's shared memories. Instead, we need to start trusting our own more. And if, for some reason, my brain may not be able to create or store strong enough autobiographical memories? Well, then it must probably from that age had to find other strategies to memorize everything I still need to have access to, to be able to handle different situations in the best way. Where one approach then surely is to try various ways to create as many "semantically episodic" memories as possible.

///

I have also written that I often focus more on other people's emotions than on my own, and that I really try to understand how I should adapt in different situations to be able to fit in the best way. I actually think that I started doing this at a very young age, but that at the age of eleven or twelve, it became increasingly intensified when I also started playing various roles to fit in, and life was becoming more difficult to understand on many levels. Apparently, I have always been a "can do it myself"-person, so then I probably had also already stopped asking questions and instead started thinking more and more by myself. And trying to handle life in that way cannot be so good all the time, and surely not so suitable in making autobiographical memories either, can it? After all, sharing our thoughts and reflections with others can also strengthen our memories, I mean.

Many years ago, I read a book by Majken Bahlenberg, and I can still recognize myself in this little girl's thoughts to this day:

> *"She did not ask. Did not want to. Did not dare. But inside, the mystery grew and she had no answer. Just knew that there was something big and difficult here that she had to listen carefully to in the faces of adults, in their voices and eyes. But first and foremost: do not ask straight out.*

Think for yourself first. And seek the answer everywhere with everyone. All the time. Carefully."

So what I have also thought about for many years is whether I might have even gone a step further in terms of this repression and role-playing, and used dissociation as a defence and a survival strategy for vast parts of my life. Because then it could perhaps mean that I have not only let "different Malin" handle different situations, but also that the various emotions ended up in separate compartments that I cannot access when I am no longer in them. This could undeniably create immense memory difficulties.

But neither that seems logical to me. For, although I believe that I have to some extent used just dissociation – both to cope with and generally be able to do as much as I did – I have probably always been well *aware* that I played various roles, albeit they have often been kept apart by almost watertight barriers, figuratively speaking. I may not remember *some* events because I have functioned like this, but that does not explain why I still have these memory difficulties to this day. Nor why pretty much my whole life seems to be erased.

/ / /

We have established that emotions make memories attach better, and in order for these emotions to be created, the help of various neurotransmitters and hormones is required. In the encoding of memories, especially dopamine, norepinephrine, adrenaline and cortisol, are very important.

Dopamine activates the brain's reward system and gives us a sense of well-being, but therefore also helps when it comes to motivating us to both learn and re-learn. Thus, store new memories or change them. We may then think especially of this when it comes to learning or changing our habits. Because we sure can often need a rich reward that motivates us to, for example, learn new (hopefully) healthier ones. But dopamine motivates us – and also helps the brain in other ways – to actually create new memories. One reason why as we get older, we can have both a slower thought pattern and more difficult to remember is just that the dopamine levels in our brain then decrease.

Otherwise, it is above all the stress hormones, adrenaline and cortisol, which in turn affect the brain to release dopamine, which really ensures that memories attach properly. Because being a little stressed actually means that we are more concentrated and focused on what is happening both with us and around us, and thus can encode stronger memories of the event. This applies to both positive and negative events. Still, we are probably most stressed when we experience something (for us) negative, and it is therefore extra important to memorize the whole thing to be able to (if possible) avoid such situations again.

But *too much* adrenaline and cortisol instead produce the opposite effect. Not only can we feel terrible – like becoming depressed or anxious – but we can also have great difficulty in both encoding and recalling memories. Yes, parts of our memory system can actually be completely knocked out if it is almost submerged in cortisol.

If we then both look at what my life has been like – that I seem to have been quite or even very stressed during large parts of it – and that I also have access to very few autobiographical memories, might indicate that my memory system has been damaged in some way due to all the stress? But neither that make sense to me, because wouldn't I then also have great difficulties when it comes to creating or recalling semantic memories? Something I don't seem to have. But this thing with stress can probably still be worth keeping in mind when I now muse further, because it may still come into play somehow.

10

How is an autobiographical memory created, and what could possibly wrong with me?

"The human brain is a wonderful organ. It starts to work as soon as you are born and doesn't stop until you get up to deliver a speech."

George Jessel

Without going into more detail on how an autobiographical memory is created, we can still start by stating that in order to have a trace, we need to be conscious and have the ability to take in different sensory impressions, and also to be able to process them. If, for example, we can neither see nor hear, the memory of an event that contains a lot of visual and auditory stimuli is likely to be meagre, to say the least. Of course, even if we lacked some sensory organs, we could still create memories. But since memories become stronger as more senses are involved during their formation, they might be more unstable and easy to eradicate. Unless powerful emotions are involved instead.

Could damage to external sensory organs or to brain areas that receive and process sensory information affect the memory's strength? This would perhaps apply in particular to visual stimuli, since vision must be quite important in creating autobiographical memories. As the saying goes, a picture says more than a thousand words.

As for myself, I have wondered if there might be some deficiencies in my visual ability, since I have virtually no access to any detailed memories at all of what my life has *looked* like. After all, I am not a visual thinker and don't have the ability to close my eyes and paint different pictures in front of me. So although I have had the physical ability to see various events, I may, for some reason, still not have managed to save them as just visual, mental images. Or maybe it is instead that I cannot now recall the images that were once created in the visual cortex? In that case, it would probably be about the latter, because even if I cannot imagine various objects or places, for example, I still recognize them when I see them again.

/ / /

The various sensory impressions we manage to process are passed on to the working memory. And if we have flaws in this memory system, it must naturally also affect the encoding of long-term memories. A great deal of other information is now also added here: parts of old memories and experiences; own thoughts and opinions about the situation we are experiencing, and perhaps concerns about how others perceive it; reflections on various courses of action and their possible consequences; information about how we feel about the whole thing, etcetera.

Here, there will be many balls to try to keep in the air simultaneously, and then it is crucial that we can focus on the most important things.

Therefore, many details may be lost here – which ones and how many depending on both the situation and ourselves – and thus never reach the long-term storage. If there is too much loss, or we miss parts essential for us to be able to create a context that is understandable to the brain – will it not mean that the memory becomes unstable and easy to erase?

I wrote earlier that I seem to pull an eraser after me, but sometimes I have also used the parable that I am like a blackboard, or nowadays it would more likely be a whiteboard, where the board eraser goes all the time, and nothing seems to be left. If I always have to be ready enough to be able to deal with all the new events that may be at the doors, I feel that I must not be too distracted by the past. And so maybe this could be where the problem is? That the sensory impressions are erased before they have been appropriately processed in my working memory? Or perhaps before they have been consolidated (strengthened) properly to be able to stick in the long-term memory? This may especially apply to visual stimuli, which, according to examination, I also seem to be hypersensitive to. Then a parable with a windscreen and its wiper blades could fit even better.

To be able to cope and be ready, the wiper blades must sweep slowly all the time, and the more visual stimuli – and then especially moving ones – the faster the blades must sweep away the impressions to keep the view clear for me. And that might mean that I don't have time to deal with even a fraction of all the information I would need to process. I also find it hard to cope with and process several sensory impressions at the same time. I can become overloaded and find it difficult to concentrate when, for example, I am exposed to too many visual and auditory stimuli at the same time. Therefore, are these imaginary wiper blades perhaps forced to do their work at the highest speed in many situations?

I could also imagine that I often tend to focus on the wrong things. Partly because I seem to lack certain filters, partly because I put so much focus on other people and their opinions, emotions and needs, in my attempts to both understand them and behave "correctly" in so many various situations. Of course, my feelings must also be in there somewhere, but maybe they often don't become conscious emotions because I push them away? Or perhaps I don't even have the ability to always notice them?

But all these emotions – both others' and my own, though perhaps sometimes repressed or unconscious – can certainly still give rise to much of the stress I have felt over the years and still feel in so many situations. And our working memory does not like to be exposed to such, because then we can very easily lose many of those balls we try to keep in the air simultaneously.

✦✦✦

Although we are talking here about *an* autobiographical memory, I would rather say that it consists of two different types of long-term memories. Namely, implicit emotional memories and explicit memories of an emotional situation. And these memories are created by the two memory systems controlled by the amygdala and hippocampus with their surrounding structures. So that we need to have well-functioning ones is therefore quite evident. If the amygdala does not work correctly, we cannot create emotional memories of the event, or at least they become very deficient. And if the hippocampus does not work correctly, we may find it hard to create any long-term memories of the event at all.

One reason why the hippocampus can be temporarily knocked out is very severe stress, as the stress hormone cortisol thus floods it – something it does not like at all. Therefore in severe trauma, for example, we cannot only get a blackout around the event itself, but also lose memories from the hours, the day, or even the days before, because they have not yet had time to consolidate. And if the negative stress is extreme or very long-lasting, the hippocampus can be seriously damaged and shrink in size as its cells die.

Now there are also several areas within the hippocampus, which in turn have slightly different functions – which I don't have much knowledge of – so any minor damage here may, depending on where they are located, at least *partially* interfere with the creation or recall of the memory. But injuries within the hippocampus can also affect, for example, our sense of direction because it is also controlled from here.

The contact *between* the amygdala and the hippocampus must naturally also work so that the memories can be created in parallel. Thus, we understand that they are both related to the event we are experiencing. Yes, what happens if they are out of sync, if at the moment, for example, we don't have access to our own feelings? Or that the focus is so intensely on the emotions of those around us that they overwhelm our own weaker emotions? Can it not be chaos in the brain when we don't really know what we are feeling, or if it genuinely is even our own feelings? And in chaos, surely it cannot be so easy for our brain to create an understandable context, which it surely needs to have access to in order to create more stable memories?

That could undoubtedly have been the case during substantial parts of my life, but I don't live in such constant chaos today. Or maybe I still do to some extent? After all, as I have said, I find it a little difficult to read myself in terms of at least some weak feelings and emotions. Not to mention putting them into words. Yes, I may actually have some trouble at all in feeling what is actually happening both with my body and within in it, so I may even find it quite tricky to tell if or when, for example, I am hungry or tired.

The fact that we have proper access to our body experiences is actually essential in creating autobiographical memories[3], because we need, among other things, a confirmation that we ourselves are experiencing an event, and no one else. And this is then especially important when it comes to being able to create really emotionally vivid memories. Because if we, for some reason, have difficulty hearing the signals from our body, our memories risk becoming very fragmentary instead.

///

---

3. See appendix for a study on this particular subject of body experience and memory.

I wrote earlier that I also often try to "switch off" certain feelings that are too painful to put up with. Or at least interfere with my ability to function in the way I think I need to be able to do in many situations. How can that be possible?

It is the prefrontal cortex – in our frontal lobes – that, in collaboration with the amygdala, controls our emotional reactions. That first processes and analyses the information from the various sensory areas, and then, based on that, plans and organizes (hopefully) appropriate feelings and actions. If this area is damaged, a large part of our emotional life will fall away, because if we don't understand that a situation requires an emotional response, nothing will happen either.

When it comes to interpreting and processing body experiences and emotions, it is the right hemisphere of our brain that is the dominant one. Instead, our left is more focused on language and logic. Hence it's also the right prefrontal cortex that triggers mainly negative emotions, such as fear and anger, while the left is instead the more analytical one, which as far as possible makes sure to subdue its right colleague so that the emotions don't grow *too* strong.

The system that interprets and processes the constantly incoming information from all corners of the body is the somatosensory system. And if damage occurs here, or the system for some reason does not work correctly, it can naturally also affect our emotional life. The most crucial area in this system in terms of emotion is what is called the insula. And suppose our right insula does not work correctly. In that case, we may have difficulty identifying and describing both our own and others' feelings and emotions; the condition known as alexithymia – something I would like to say that I have to some extent.

So perhaps my "shutdown ability" could be explained by the fact that my left prefrontal cortex has quite a lot of power over its right colleague, and thus so often has the ability to dampen its attempts at emotional reactions? Unless they have become too powerful or complex, that is.

Or maybe it could be that the right side, for some reason, may have some difficulty when it comes to both sending signals to and receiving them from the somatosensory system and amygdala? It is not only the hippocampus that can be damaged by prolonged, negative stress; it can also be the prefrontal cortex. For example, it has been seen that some people who have PTSD have reduced activity in a specific part of the prefrontal cortex and, therefore, may have difficulty dealing with strong emotions. Now that rhymes badly with my ability to shut down, but maybe the area may have been damaged in some other way? And where then perhaps mainly the right side has been taken its toll?

But my possible disturbances can perhaps even be found already in the somatosensory system and then especially in the insula. Because as I said, I can often have difficulty really reading both my body and my emotions. In any case, could all these examples mean that my map of different body states might not always be as clear and informative as it would need to be, to help create strong and lasting autobiographical memories?

Then memories also need to be consolidated (strengthened) and stored properly. And then sleep is crucial because that is when memories are primarily consolidated. But it should also be said that sleep is essential even before it is time for this memory storage. Yes, among other things, the hippocampus first wants the opportunity to clear out all old information and make room for this new memory. However, the fact is that our *whole* brain is cleaned during sleep: the cerebrospinal fluid that surrounds it then takes care of rinsing off all the nooks and crannies really well. Therefore, sleep deprivation is not at all good if we want the memory to attach in the best way. No, surely it should instead lead to a more unstable memory that can be more easily erased?

I cannot say that I do sleep well, and I probably had even more significant difficulties when my mother was ill. But above all, I usually slept woefully bad when I was struggling as well as I could in my contact with psychiatry, and especially when I was hospitalized, a time during which I barely slept at all. However, I have always been well aware that sleep is vital. And I have also valued (and value) it immensely, because if there is something I have wanted to do over the years, it has been just to sleep away from all the hard work. I know, for example, that I always tried to make sure that my mother – when she was not feeling well – got into bed and got the sleep she so badly needed, which far from always went so well. But I also know that I myself tried to sleep whenever I got a chance, which could likely mean that it sometimes had to be during the day. The fact that this way, I still managed to get quite a lot of sleep during those years probably contributed to me actually having the strength and ability to do as much as I did, after all. And that I was as good as I was at school.

✦✦✦

But even if it is mainly during sleep that memories are consolidated, to some extent, they also seem to do so at rest. Something that we allow our brain to do very much, almost half of our waking time. However, it should be pointed out that "rest" is a misleading word, because our brain works even when we don't more actively give it problems to solve. And just like during the night's consolidation, the prefrontal cortex and hippocampus are then active, and so is the area of the angular gyrus, to which I will return shortly. They are namely all part of the network that works for us when we rest, known as the default mode network (DMN).

When we do things routinely – which we usually do – or maybe just sit down and take it easy, our brain takes the opportunity to go on walks. We then let the thoughts wander freely or daydream. Perhaps these thoughts are about ourselves, our surroundings, and what is happening in our lives right now, but most often, our brain takes us on journeys both backwards and forwards in time. And, of course, it can also paint pure fantasy scenes. That our brain is allowed to wander and daydream like this strengthens our memories to some extent, but above all, it helps us when it comes to planning for our future and in problem-solving. And on top of that, it can also give our creative thinking an extra boost. But, even in these different tasks, sleep is still our most important tool.

Memories are thus strengthened even when we think about and reflect on them. Now I obviously don't remember how much I have reflected on different events in my life, but I have probably thought more about certain things, and others I have instead had to turn away from me in order to survive. I still believe that I have usually thought a lot, but since, at the same time, there have always been so many various things to keep track of and try to keep apart, maybe my brain has not been able to process everything? And then perhaps, above all, things that have concerned my own feelings and needs have had to be sacrificed?

✸✸✸

However, the consolidation process must undoubtedly be disrupted in many other ways as well, which means that the brain cannot process the different parts of memory in a way that provides a more stable trace. What happens, for example, if the prefrontal cortex does not come into contact with the emotional parts of the amygdala, or they are too contradictory? Will the consolidation continue then, or will the memory be increasingly erased instead? I may have saved emotional images created from both myself and others.

As I said, I have also played (and am playing) many different roles in my life, and have often really tried to keep them apart with almost watertight barriers. Could that perhaps have disrupted the consolidation? Maybe it cannot be so easy for the brain to keep all those roles apart when they are still together on the same body?

My life has also been filled to the brim with so much I have not understood, which many times would not even have been possible to understand, in terms of, for example, my mum's illness, my relationship with other people and what I have tried to achieve together with psychiatry. And when we think about (seemingly) incomprehensible things, it can undeniably lead to chaos in our brain, which surely cannot be a good breeding ground for creating more stable memories?

Therefore, in addition to thinking about the events, we may also need to talk about them with someone else. Someone who may be able to help us both better understand what we have experienced and find other points of view when it comes to reflecting further on it. Unfortunately, I didn't have anyone to talk to about everything that was difficult during my mother's illness – apart from my brother, but he was probably spared most of my thoughts – until I turned to psychiatry. It could naturally have played some part in my lack of memories from those years. But since I have had someone to talk to since the age of 25, surely that should have meant that my memory has also slowly but surely begun to improve? Which it does not seem to have done.

Otherwise, just talking is very important to me when it comes to memorizing things, and I don't even have to speak to someone else every time. For things I put into words, I remember better, and especially if I also hear the words pronounced. It will then be semantic memories – or "semantically episodic" – but I will have to grab what I have the opportunity to get, I guess.

///

Of course, the lack of access to autobiographical memories does not have to be solely due to the fact that these memories have not even been created. It may also be the case that, for some reason, we don't have the ability to recall them.

When we remember a previous event, the brains network created by the two memory systems in the current event is (hopefully) activated again. We can then, if all goes well, paint a picture within us, or even a film that consists of, for example, visual, auditory and sensory images. And we can also be filled with a feeling (or more than one) associated with the event we look back on.

From what I understand, a really vivid memory is usually also very detailed. Because unless all these details are added, the memory will not only be vaguer, but it will probably also be much harder to get the feeling that something has actually happened to us. Instead of a memory seen from a first-person perspective, it becomes more of a third-person view. It thus becomes very difficult to get that feeling of reliving the event, the resonance in the body, which is the very definition of an autobiographical memory.

The fact that this seems to be the case has been seen in some studies involving people with damage to a specific area of the brain, or where the area has been temporarily "knocked out" with the help of so-called transcranial magnetic stimulation. The area in question is the angular gyrus of the left hemisphere, which according to some researchers, is believed to be responsible for the contextual details of memory – while the hippocampus is then rather responsible for the more basic context.

Since the hippocampus was not affected in these studies, the individuals didn't entirely lose their autobiographical memory. Still, the memories became significantly poorer and were more difficult to paint as living images.

But all these images, which are created from the inside, are in any case just very fleeting reconstructions and therefore never as solid and clear as those made by impressions we take to ourselves from the outside. Our memories become rather pale copies, although there are exceptions such as traumatic memories. And if the memories that I may still managed to create for some reason from the beginning were very fragmentary, will that mean that the reconstructions will be even paler copies? Yes, maybe so faint that they are barely visible? And do these memories then slowly but surely disappear further and further into the fog I leave behind when I stumble forward here in life?

And suppose I now sometimes have a hard time registering what I really feel in different situations in "real life". In that case, it may mean that I may have even more difficulty getting in touch with certain emotions that should be associated with those *I know that*-memories I still have access to. Maybe that is why they don't resonate at all in my body? But surely, it could just as easily be due to the almost total lack of contextual details in these memories. Yes, the latter is probably a much more likely explanation, I think.

In "real life", various events also take place over much more extended periods of time, in contrast to the short neural activity that occurs when we remember a memory. So for me, who can sometimes need plenty of time to process information, maybe this time factor can be crucial and mean that my memories become too faded?

Even when recalling memories, as we have previously stated, stress can put its spanner in the works for us, as stress affects both the hippocampus and the prefrontal cortex, and also makes us focus more on how we have it here and now than helps us look back on something we have already experienced. At least if these are situations in which we have been in entirely different states of mind from our current situation. If the memory is also a pale copy, or even a very pale one, well, then perhaps it does not take much stress for it to become almost impossible to get hold of? And that I am probably at least a little stressed, although I am not always even aware of it, in the vast majority of situations we can likely establish. For life is usually anything but a bed of roses.

11

Memories of the future

"Memories are the key not to the past, but to the future."

Corrie ten Boom

The most important task of the autobiographical memory system may be to help us create "memories of the future" (that is, give us ideas about the future), so we should probably think a bit about this as well. As I said, I have a hard time even when it comes to creating "memories of the future", and especially when it comes to imagining myself in this future, something that creates a constant feeling of insecurity. Therefore this difficulty generates worry, yes, sometimes even severe anxiety. But it also depresses me when, for example, I cannot imagine a happier future in moments when I feel bad, or life is extra hard. Feelings that are anything but pleasant to have to deal with. Hence it would be so nice if I could find some way to change this – although unfortunately, I find it hard to believe that it can be possible.

After all, "memories of the future" are created by our already existing memories – conscious as well as unconscious – and all the knowledge we possess, and then linked to a feeling that we ourselves will be part of this future. So even alexithymia (the difficulty of interpreting one's own and others' feelings and emotions) can put a spanner in the works in our creation of memories like these. And so can the condition that is called aphantasia, which consists of not having the ability to visualize images in the head; to have a blind inner eye. But the fact is that the ability to imagine other impressions is most often also decreased in other sensory domains – and some individuals even have a complete lack of multi-sensory imagery – such as envisioning how something sounds, tastes, feels, etcetera. And apart from that, some aphantasic individuals also have trouble with facial recognition.

Experiences, dreams, desires, needs, feelings, thoughts and reflections are thus mixed together in a single mess, and out of this can come all sorts of possible (and impossible) "memories of the future". Many of them we use daily, while others may never be real – because, for example, we will never be able to afford that dream trip if we don't win the lottery. As long as I cannot access my autobiographical memories, and also have both aphantasia and, to some extent, alexithymia, I probably will not be able to create more vivid "memories of the future" either. But these will likely continue to be meagre *I know that*-memories. Which I thus manage to create with the help of routines and logical thinking.

As I mentioned in the previous chapter, we daydream a large part of our waking time, and these thoughts and dreams are not only memories of the past but are just as often "memories of the future". The hippocampus is, of course, involved and necessary in both memory processes. Studies have shown that although hippocampus injuries don't seem to affect the number of mental journeys, daydreams' content and shape will still be slightly different. And the descriptions of these fit very well with what I experience. (Although I would like to add that I hardly daydream at all; once it is calm up in the office, there is usually quite empty and black.)

My thoughts are usually rooted in the present or the near future. And they are also of a semantic nature – fact-based rather than emotionally episodic – and almost entirely verbal (linguistic). When I sit and think, I don't paint visual images but instead have a conversation with myself. And the very few images I can still paint once in a while, even if they then become incredibly diffuse, are in the form of patterns or drawings. For example, if I were to try to paint a house's image, it would at best be a highly unclear drawing of how some of the rooms might be located. Thus, no details or shapes and colours.

My few "memories of the future" are thus almost exclusively very close in time – days rather than months or years – and they are verbal. For example, it may be about different theories about what might happen in an imminent situation, and thoughts on how I should then act and what I should say. But I cannot "paint" any detailed scenes in front of me; but instead, I talk to myself about what they might possibly look like. I try to have a logical and theoretical reasoning based on the facts available to me.

However, the details – to which I have virtually no access whatsoever – in our memories are not the most important thing when it comes to creating effective "memories of the future". Or to be able to deal with the present at all. No, the essential thing is instead the general experience and the different emotional memories we have accumulated throughout our lives. Because knowing how we feel about various objects and situations is what can help us the most in life. And I am then thinking in particular of all situations that constantly arise in the personal and social spheres.

I still have access to general experiences to a certain extent, but unfortunately, it is a little worse with those feelings that could help me take care of myself in the best way. And in the long run, also help me in contact with other people. That is, the knowledge and experience of my own feelings and needs.

♦ ♦

Speaking of memories and "memories of the future", the neurologist Antonio Damasio has, in my opinion, a fascinating theory about something he calls somatic markers. These markers could perhaps be considered as parts of our autobiographical memory, springing from our own experiences. They are placed on our inner body map, and make themselves felt in the form of a feeling – conscious or not – when we consider decisions or actions in different situations.

Somatic markers thus help us sift through all the countless options and possible consequences that actually arise from very many decisions we make daily, but which we probably don't always even think about because they often work in silence. They raise the alarm at choices that are (probably) negative for us, to instead focus on those that are (probably) more positive. These conscious markers can make themselves known as feelings of what we like or not, what scares us or not, what we consider to be right or wrong, etcetera. While the unconscious ones instead give a gut feeling or perhaps an even vaguer intuition about which choice, decision or action is probably the best thing for ourselves – and our surroundings – in a particular situation.

Some of these somatic markers are already there when we are born because they are required for our survival, such as hunger when blood sugar falls or that we flinch away when an object does the same. But we still collect the vast majority of them during the course of our lives. They arise in the brain as a result of innate preferences, upbringing, education and cultural influence.

Some specific types of stimuli have thus gradually become associated with certain specific body conditions. Therefore, when they appear in different situations, they can quickly advise us, so that we don't have to get caught up in endless thinking and analysis of various options and all their possible consequences. It is namely the case that we would run the risk of becoming over-rational without access to our feelings and experiences. In the vast majority of situations, something that is absolutely not for our benefit, at least not in the personal and social spheres.

♦♦♦

Damasio gives an example from his own practice, where a patient with injuries to the prefrontal cortex came to the laboratory on a winter day. The patient had driven a car and told them completely undisturbed that there had been no problems whatsoever, despite the glass-slippery roads. He had calmly made his way because he had followed the rules to follow, while other motorists had instead panicked and edged off the road. In this case, therefore, the patient's lack of somatic markers was to his advantage, unlike his fellow road users. However, when he was due to make a new appointment with Damasio the next day, this shortcoming became anything but appropriate. The patient then analysed the different options *ad absurdum*, so in the end, Damasio simply had to decide for him.

Feelings and emotions can thus cause problems sometimes, but without them, we would be anything but well-functioning. Regrettably, I have to admit that I recognize to some extent what is described above, although I absolutely don't have as much trouble as this patient. Because I can actually be quite calm and focused in certain situations, which for others may be both scary and stressful, but can then almost get wholly stuck when it comes to something as simple as, for example, determine a new time with some caregiver. Or maybe decide which pants to put on, if I have not already decided that the day before.

/ / /

These somatic markers are mainly created during our childhood and youth, although we naturally continue to create them with the help of emotional experiences throughout our lives. So what happens if, even at a very young age, you started to put as much focus on other people as I seem to have done? More focus on their reactions, needs, desires, etcetera than on my own. And gradually began to imitate others more and more and then also began to play various roles in different situations. Could this not mean that I may have misplaced at least some somatic markers, more based on the surroundings' expectations and needs? Although they have been created with the help of my own feelings, perhaps these could have arisen instead because of my feelings of the surroundings, not from my own experience of the different situations or objects?

Then came my mum's illness with all the extreme emotions, and also psychiatry with its opinions on how most of us people function and what we feel good about (or not). And I did my very best to adapt to both situations. Yes, sadly, I even used violence on myself in trying to fit in in the best way. Surely it may have caused even more problems when it comes to creating somatic markers, especially since my brain also must have tried to create them even based on my own needs? And in that case, perhaps the attempts to read this somewhat diffuse body map and all these emotions maybe even caused some confusion? Like when, for example, it comes to the ability to create unified, autobiographical memories?

But although it probably does not affect the ability to create memories to any great extent, it is undoubtedly still not good to create too many somatic markers based on our surroundings' emotions, expectations, and needs. No, we also need to have at least access to a really solid set of markers based solely on our own experience. And then also to have the ability to keep these different markers apart in some way.

//

In any case, I think that we can state that it is essential that we have access to our feelings and experiences. I notice myself how hard it is when I don't always have this access. When I don't really know how I feel in different situations, or how I will feel if I decide to deal with any of them; and what that, in turn, might give rise to and how best to deal with it; and how…

All these new stages, which constantly follow the previous ones, can sometimes cause my brain to spin. And surely that is when it would be darn good to have access to at least that part of the autobiographical memory that I, like Damasio, have now chosen to call somatic markers?

Still, I actually have access to a lot of such, although, as I said, they are often more associated with the expectations, needs and desires of others. Which naturally is something that is also good to have access to in many situations. For example, when it comes to responding to and helping other people, I can often get that gut feeling that can lead me right. And in recent years, I have slowly but surely also managed to place more and more of my own markers, which in at least some situations tell me which decisions will probably be the best to make based on my own needs and desires.

12

So what have we come up with?

"There are things known and there are things unknown, and in between are the doors of perception."

Aldous Huxley

The fact that I have now had the opportunity to write down my thoughts like this has been beneficial to me. And that is even though sometimes it has been quite painful to do so. Putting together so many of my thoughts has not only meant that I had had the opportunity to process some of what I have been through, but it has also brought with it the fact that entirely new insights have emerged. Ideas that I have then also been able to share, especially with Nouchine Hadjikhani. Because while I have been working on this text and musing here in my solitude, researchers also have thought about the subject. And all these thoughts have since also led to a case report of my autobiographical memory difficulties. An article that I will soon return to briefly.

In addition to the fact that this has been so useful to me, I also hope that I have at least to some extent been able to answer the question of what it means to lack autobiographical memory. That I have been able to convey some descriptions of what it is like to walk in my shoes. Descriptions that may then also have created recognition for those of

225

you with similar difficulties – and at least some understanding among those of you who are instead lucky enough to have a well-functioning memory.

Although my knowledge is still far from as great as I would like it to be, I still feel that I have now started to get at least the basics more and more clear to me. Both in terms of how our autobiographical memory is structured and what can affect it, and – not least – what deficiencies seem to exist with me. During my musing, I have concluded that there must be many different ailments and problems, in addition to injuries and diseases of the brain, which can also bring with them some memory difficulties. Cognitive problems, perceptual disorders, alexithymia, depression, stress, anxiety and difficulty sleeping are just a few of them, I would think.

I have also realized that some brains already seem to be fundamentally differently connected and therefore don't have a completely "normal" functioning memory system, be it an ability to remember too much or too little. And if we look at a functional variant such as autism, some studies have shown that the signals and connections within, for example, DMN[4] seem to work somewhat differently. If that is the case, I think that many other autistic people may also have some difficulties getting hold of their autobiographical memories – but perhaps even more so, at least have the condition aphantasia.

///

---

4. See appendix for a brief description of the network.

But if we then go to me and the difficulties I have, would we now be able to draw any conclusions? Have I, for example, found in my own musings some reasons I think to be more likely than others as to why I have these memory problems? No, not in detail, of course. But as I said, I think I have started to get at least the basics set for me now.

First of all, I think I must have had this memory impairment with me since childhood, because I find it very difficult to make it logically all fit together otherwise. I believe that my brain fundamentally functions somewhat differently and has done so throughout my life, and that my memory difficulties have not arisen through either an injury or caused by the events I have been through. But sure, they may have gotten worse because of these events and experiences. Stress, anxiety and difficulty sleeping are, as we have established, after all, not a good breeding ground for the creation of memories.

Over the years, I have also believed that emotions and body experiences must have a player, or maybe even several, included in the game here. That for some reason, I may not be able to fully notice all the signals from the body map that my brain has most certainly both created and constantly keeps up to date. But now that I have considered it further, I think that these potential difficulties in noticing signals, or if for some reason they are not appropriately transmitted, could naturally also be found in some other areas of the brain that are important for our autobiographical memories. And if so, is it somewhere within the DMN that any of these signal deviations can be found? Thus, the network that includes, among others, the medial prefrontal cortex, hippocampus and angular gyrus.

Previously, I have not thought that there could be anything significantly wrong with my hippocampus. After all, I can both create semantic memories and have at least a reasonably good sense of direction. But now that I have thought more and read so many different studies, I have had to rethink a little. Because if we see to that, I not only find it unmanageable to remember my past but also hard to create "memories of the future", and that both the content and form of my reflections in daydreams seem to be different from the "normal", then surely that must suggest at least some minor disturbance there? Which either interferes with the creation and consolidation of memories or makes me unable to recall them.

And since I also have such great difficulty remembering details – recalling virtually none at all – I actually think that there is somehow a lack when it comes to processing, storing or reminiscing memories created primarily by visual stimuli. As I wrote earlier, I have over the years wondered if I might even have some deficiencies in my visual ability, and that the flaws might be in the visual cortex, for example. But I guess I have pretty much put that thought aside now. If the theories I have raised here are correct, I would instead guess that it may be a problem with the angular gyrus, which has very close contact with both the visual and auditory cortex. Maybe my (left) angular gyrus cannot handle all its tasks properly, at least not those that involve registering or saving contextual details?

///

Instead, let us move on to the researchers' thoughts about my predicaments and what they might be due to.

First, they had to try to establish that I actually have memory difficulties. This was done using a test to measure my ability to recreate autobiographical memories of specific episodes in my life. During a couple of hours of conversation with a researcher, I was therefore tasked with trying to date and place the different memories that might appear when he read out various words, and then also try to describe the memory as detailed as possible. Unsurprisingly, my test result was deplorable, and not even the very emotionally charged memories I still managed to get to some extent seemed to have any good autobiographical quality.

Of course, my brain has also been examined in different ways; with MRI, MEG and EEG, both its appearance and its activity have been studied. The findings made don't contradict my own thoughts regarding deviations in, for example, the structures hippocampus and angular gyrus. No – on the contrary.

Among other things, it was found that my hippocampus is smaller than other women of my age on both sides, but in addition that my right hippocampus is significantly smaller than the left one. (Something that Palombo et al. also found in the individuals in their SDAM study from 2015.) A volume difference that was not found in the same-aged women in the control group. Signal abnormalities were also found in a few different brain areas, in the form of epileptiform activity, and one area where such activity was found was the left angular gyrus. But abnormalities were also found in my left temporal lobe and in the two occipital lobes (where the visual cortex is located). The researchers also raised concerns about this kind of memory problem's possible connections to autism. Thoughts that I myself have had and still have. But more detailed descriptions of the researchers' findings can be found in the article "A case report of severely impaired autobiographical memory in a woman with Asperger syndrome." (Hadjikhani et al.) at the end of this book.[5]

***

Personally, I believe that I will have to deal with these memory difficulties for the rest of my life, but I really wish it could be changed somehow. Yes, I would be immensely grateful if someone said it could be corrected and, in that case, also explained how. But as it is probably not possible to do anything about it, I am still grateful to have at least begun to get hold of an explanation of how it could be like this. Or at least have gained more knowledge about where there seem to be deficiencies in my brain that could explain these predicaments.

***

I would also like to raise something else I have thought more and more about during my writing. Something I believe to be very important and well worth emphasizing. Firstly, I think that at least caregivers should try to take memory problems like these more seriously, even though they may not be able to understand them or hardly believe

---

5. See appendix.

them. Because if I as a patient take courage and really try to present such, in my opinion, tormenting difficulties, which can be both very frightening and shameful, well, then I certainly think that I at least deserve to be listened to properly and that what I (or anyone else in the same situation) say should also be taken seriously.

What I also think is extremely important to consider when meeting with patients is to acknowledge that some can fundamentally function differently, even in other ways. That there may be biological reasons for acting in a certain way, and that the treatment or advice that suits most other patients in seemingly similar situations may therefore not fit this time. No, it may even do more harm than good, which sadly very much has come to do in my case.

In psychiatry, one can sometimes be told that the diagnosis itself is not so important. Or at least that as a patient, you should not care so much as it is only a work tool for the caregivers in which one's difficulties and symptoms are described. After all, a good caregiver should first and foremost see and respond to the patient, not to the diagnosis. And of course, I agree with this to some extent because, as a patient, one wants to be treated as a human being rather than as a diagnosis. But although the idea of diagnoses was once only to be descriptions of symptoms, they don't really work like that today. No, there is often also a thought about how the patient function, and sometimes even what may be behind it and what should then be done about it.

So to make a diagnosis that, although it describes a lot of symptoms, gives an incorrect picture of how the patient function can be devastating. And not only because you as a patient are at risk of being treated incorrectly, but also because you risk looking at yourself and your difficulties in a worse way. Because a diagnosis can actually be a tool even for the patient, which can help understand oneself and one's problems and find ways to deal with them. Hence it is essential that such one must be as accurate and well descriptive as possible.

Of course, I am well aware that it can be complicated to diagnose autism, especially in women. And I fully understand that psychiatry didn't even think about, for example, Asperger's syndrome when I first sought help. Because the official criteria for that diagnosis didn't even exist then, they were described sometime in the early 90s. The fact that I have a family history that has also affected my well-being, and which was already well known by psychiatry, naturally meant that it was logical to start by searching for the answers there. Yes, to some extent, I, too, probably thought that if I could just sort that out, the other pieces of the puzzle I was looking for would probably also fall into place.

But as time went on and I just came to feel worse, surely psychiatry should have understood, or at least started to think about, that it must be about something else as well. Yes, I have to say that I think so. And I certainly think that it should have been at least apparent during the neuropsychological evaluation, because there, if somewhere, knowledge about autism should exist. But instead of finally getting help with both understanding my difficulties and finding better strategies to deal with them, I was told that "no recommendation for further action" could be made. Something that cannot be said to be entirely optimal, can it? I also think that there should be a better basic knowledge of

NPD (neuropsychiatric disorders) in general in psychiatry. And that *all* caregivers – not just doctors and psychologists – would then also have a responsibility to question a patient's diagnosis when it does not seem to be correct.

⫽⫽⫽

Now I feel once again that both fear and feelings of shame and guilt come crawling here, just as they have done several times during my writing, because I have now expressed myself a little negatively about psychiatry in several places. But at the same time, I feel that I actually need to be able to do just that if I am to have a chance to try to convey both experiences and thoughts about my difficulties in an honest way.

However, this does *not* mean that I am not at the same time well aware that most of the people I have come across in psychiatry have most likely done their best to both help and support me. Something I am also incredibly grateful for, of course. Yes, several of the people I had contact with for a long time even came to mean a lot to me. But no matter how much I have tried, and still try to, embrace, adapt and value *all* the help, explanations and supportive advice given to me in all good faith, the fact remains that so many times, it has only come to hurt worse.

These are words and feelings I would rather disown, as they make me feel so mean and ungrateful. But unfortunately, it is a truth I still think I need to try to say out loud sometimes, even though I get this scared and stressed once I do. Because it is as Gunilla Gerland writes:

"Other people's good intentions were always harder for me to deal with emotionally than their dislike or anger. Well-meaning actions were painful, because they were always wrong in some way; no one ever saw my real problems."

"I was unable to have my feelings confirmed anywhere, so I presumed the others were right."

///

But even though it is now so terribly painful to have these memory difficulties, and I thus would do almost anything to get rid of them, there are maybe also some positive things. Perhaps, for example, I would feel even worse from all the painful and frightening things I have experienced if I had had access to all the details and feelings? Apparently, my grandmother often used the saying: "Every cloud has a silver lining." And maybe there is something in it anyway?

On the other hand, I would then be able to remember much of all the fine things I have experienced and many of the exciting and interesting meetings I have been through. Not to mention all the people who have been a part of my life. Thus, things that could have compensated for the more tormenting memories. Yes, then I probably would have at least been able to feel "real" and have had more proper access to my "I"? And I also might have been able to put more value on and feel true joy over things that can be good in this life after all?

But unfortunately, these are questions I will never get any answers to, I guess.

Afterword

"There is only one cardinal rule: One must always listen to the patient."

Oliver Sacks

After some books had already been printed, I felt that it might also be appropriate to insert an afterword, where I briefly tell you a little about what happened next in, among other things, my contact with psychiatry.

After the autism diagnosis and even the referral to the habilitation had been rejected, it just increasingly felt like I was allowed to keep my conversational contact at the psychiatric clinic out of mercy. Something that was very stressful, especially as the contact with the nurse had not felt especially good at any time (absolutely no offence meant!). It had always felt as if I didn't quite reach her, that there was a glass wall I could not force, and that there was no genuine interest in my difficulties either.

It was said that after the habilitation assessment, I would meet with the psychiatrist at the clinic again to try to ascertain what help possibly could be offered to me. But that didn't happen, first because of changes associated with the coronavirus, and then because the doctor quit. So it was not until eight months later that a meeting with a new psychiatrist took place. A meeting I felt anything but good about. Not to mention how bad I came to feel from the following medical record notes, messages and things the doctor did. If one does not have either the understanding or the will to listen appropriately, one can, by what one says, writes and does, cause very great harm to a patient. Especially if a patient, like me, has already been hurt very badly by psychiatry for so long. I thus asked also to have my own messages included in the medical record, but nope. So the caregivers' words were once again standing for the whole truth – despite inaccuracies and omitted information – which frightens me.

During this long wait, I had given my book to the clinic. But I had also more intensively tried to explain to the nurse how painful my significant memory impairment is, and how incredibly sad and lonely I feel when others find it so difficult to understand them. Yes, that even psychiatry does not seem to want to try to do it. And when I later took courage and asked if anyone had read my book - and admittedly got a yes, but no more response than that - I felt that it was probably high time to end the contact. Which, after three more visits and attempts to reach her, I did. I had already asked, and now I did it once again, if there was anyone else at the clinic who might then be more interested in learning a little about NPD[6] and memory difficulties - and got the answer that there probably was not.

This was also something I got confirmed after meeting with the psychiatrist, and after she had asked the clinic team to raise the question of

---

6. Neuropsychiatric disorders.

whether it was possible to change nurse, and was told "no". She also wrote a new referral to the habilitation, which also received a quick and concise rejection. In the attempts to still find some form of support, I changed medical centre (because the psychologist I met at the habilitation now works there) and called there crying and asking for help. But no, I was not allowed to go there either because I belong in specialist care. I was already feeling horrible, but now the situation became almost unendurable. Yes, for example, I lost five kilos in a few weeks because the treatment and all uncertainty made me so stressed and terrified that all too often, I just cried and vomited alternately.

I now understand that I was naive in my belief that with a new diagnosis and so much knowledge, I might finally get the support I need based on the difficulties (but also strengths) and needs I have. But unfortunately, it has rather been turned against me, as a way of writing me off and instead be able to refer me to someone else. And to continue to belittle me.

I find it absurd that the psychiatric clinic does not have more knowledge about NPD, but even more outrageous that they don't even seem to want to learn. For example, *I* have a lot of knowledge about myself and the difficulties I have, which I am happy to share if only someone shows a genuine interest in listening and trying to understand. Unfortunately, however, this interest does not seem to exist, and it feels both painful and strange. If they don't want to try to understand their patients, why do they work in psychiatry?

✝ ✝ ✝

This Kafkaesque contact with psychiatry has hurt me *very* badly. Yes, I have barely managed to fight on. But thankfully, I have continued contact with GNC, where especially Nouchine Hadjikhani has truly helped me keep my head above the surface. But I have also talked to Christopher Gillberg, and later we also had a video meeting where the three of us jointly thought about where support might be found. Christopher contacted the habilitation psychiatrist, but I was not surprised by yet another rejection; just resigned and despairing. I was then transferred back to the psychiatric clinic, to the NPD team's psychiatrist, for "further assessment and follow-up". Now I was so stressed out that I had to fight hard against the urge to end my life. I was not informed either but found the information in my medical record. After my own pressure and another two months of waiting, I was finally told that I stood in line for a psychiatrist meeting. But to be honest, I don't think it will lead to anything good. I simply have neither faith nor hope in psychiatry any longer. But let us hope that I am wrong.

Sadly, I was not wrong, although I had a good first meeting with the psychiatrist, where he promised to speak with both the head of his own clinic and the habilitation about my needs and possibilities to find a solution. After another three months of waiting, I was hence invited to a video meeting with the NPD team's and habilitation's psychiatrists, where they put forward some other suggestions for help and treatment. Things I don't need and also would feel terrible about.

Here the meeting really turned into some kind of torture for me (just like the following awful medical record notes) when the two psychiatrists considered me to be rigid when I stuck to the need I have. And they also thought that I had deficiencies in both theory of mind and cognitive empathy, and that I didn't understand their perspective. Which I certainly did, but I still had to stick to my knowledge and needs, even if no support could be offered. If there was anyone who had flaws in cognitive empathy here, it was the psychiatrists, who had no ability whatsoever to understand what it is like to walk in my shoes. And the greatest rigidity is actually found in the healthcare system, and not in me – or in other patients who, like me, are struggling in this system.

A few weeks later, I had a follow-up phone call with the NPD team's psychiatrist, during which, despite severe anxiety and fear, I again tried to very clearly present both my own needs and how important I consider it to be to try to understand patients' situations. I also mentioned what is stated in the paragraph above in terms of rigidity and cognitive empathy. And I also stressed how important I think it is that both psychiatry and habilitation try to acquire at least some knowledge about SDAM and aphantasia, especially since the latter condition seems to be quite common in autistic people.

But I felt that I didn't get a good response, and indeed there were no notes on the above mentioned in my medical record either. Instead, the focus was once again on how dissatisfied I am with psychiatry's and habilitation's suggestions, treatments and medical record notes. Unfortunately, the two instances seem to have great difficulty with self-reflection. Something I find very frightening and sad, because all the faults and flaws are certainly not only to be found in their patients.

Although the support I need could not be offered, it would have been both helpful and nice to have at least received some form of confirmation. That someone had endeavoured to express a few words of regret over that I have had to suffer so badly (and for such a long time) in psychiatry. But nope. So here again, the big, black hole opened up in front of me, which – despite knowing better – I stepped right out into. A hole not only filled with exceedingly great sorrow, but unfortunately, also with great shame over myself.

I thus ended my contact with the psychiatric clinic, because I honestly don't have the energy to fight in the attempts to be understood anymore. So instead, I now have to try once again to find both the will and strength to be able to search for support and help elsewhere.

✦ ✦ ✦

As for my somatic problems, I was well treated at Akademiska in Uppsala. However, the neurologist dismissed dystonia and instead considered something similar to, for example, Stiff Person Syndrome. But since I have already taken samples in the attempts to exclude the disease, we came to the conclusion that it may then rather be a Malin Syndrome. A constant muscle tension state that we (at present) don't know what it is due to. However, it was decided that I should be treated with the same medications, namely relatively high doses of benzodiazepines in the form of Clonazepam. Although I still have some painful problems with mainly the neck, chest, and diaphragm, my legs have become much softer and more stable, which I am pleased about because I can then walk more again.

A few concluding words

Writing this has thus been very useful for me, and I hope that it has also given you, as a reader, at least something. But of course, I wish I had had the ability to write about my experiences differently. That I could really have shared the thoughts, experiences and feelings I have had over the years. I mean that I wish I could have written a more "ordinary" autobiography. But if you, like me, have an autobiographical memory problem, you know that this cannot be done so easily.

Now there are thankfully many women who not only have access to their autobiographical memories but who also are absolutely fantastic writers. So if you want to read more about, for example, autism and how important it is to be correctly diagnosed, I can recommend, for instance, Gunilla Gerland's "A Real Person: Life on the Outside". An excellent and strong autobiography that has meant a lot to me. I can also recommend three other good biographies, namely "Pretending to be Normal" by Liane Holliday Willey, "Drama Queen" by Sara Gibbs, and "I Overcame my Autism and all I Got Was this Lousy Anxiety Disorder" by Sarah Kurchak. The latter two are also very humorous.

♦ ♦ ♦

As I have already written, there is a lack of information about the memory problem that has come to be known as Severely Deficient Autobiographical Memory (SDAM). However, on this website, there is still a lot of helpful information to read: http://sdamstudy.weebly.com/.

And here you will find people's experiences and thoughts about this condition (yes, even a link to a podcast), but you can also contribute yourself: https://www.reddit.com/r/SDAM/.

Another condition that usually (or perhaps rather always) goes hand in hand with SDAM is aphantasia (to have a blind inner eye), and more information about it can be found on this page: https://aphantasia.com/ and on YouTube: https://www.youtube.com/c/AphantasiaNetwork. On Reddit, you can find this: https://www.reddit.com/r/Aphantasia/. And on YouTube, you can also find another informative channel, by Alan Kendle: https://youtu.be/1DNpMBkW8k8.

I have noticed that what is written and said often takes place from a relatively positive perspective. Something I myself don't succeed at all with concerning my own SDAM and aphantasia. So, unfortunately, what I take part of can thus often fill me with both sadness and great self-loathing. Then it is crucial to try to remember (and preferably also get support) that how you are affected by the conditions depends so much on one's personality and the possible other difficulties one has, and on what one's family life, work and social networks look like, etcetera. Something I think is usually forgotten in the texts and interviews I read.

☙☙☙

The notes from my medical record are directly quoted in the Swedish edition, but naturally slightly changed in this book due to the translation. I have chosen to exclude the names of caregivers and have also spelt out abbreviations.

Acknowledgements

First of all, I would like to express my sincere thanks to Professor Nouchine Hadjikhani. Because not only did she get me to write this book and contributed with both feedback and fact-checking, but she also assisted me through thick and thin throughout the whole writing process – and is there as a huge support for me still: Your feedback, your infinite patience and your warm concern have both been and are truly invaluable to me!

Of course, I would also like to thank Professor Christopher Gillberg, who already when we first met, encouraged me to write down my thoughts and reflections. Besides, he immediately understood that it was not about a personality disorder in me, and also became interested in and took my memory problems seriously: Thank you for your understanding, and that I finally got diagnoses that now also help *me* understand myself better!

I would also like to express my thanks to my two psychologists:

Margareta, who stood by me for so many years and also helped me to make the (for me) vital contact with Christopher Gillberg and the Gillberg Neuropsychiatry Centre. During my writing, she too contributed with, for example, information and feedback regarding trauma and EMDR treatment: Thank you for your great support and all the help you gave me!

Inger, who had the strength to stand by my side for so many years. Something that we probably both are having a hard time understanding today. With her support, I was still able to get through the toughest and most painful years in psychiatry, and thus I have now been able to write this book. Besides, she wrote very detailed medical record notes, which I have significantly benefited from here: Thank you for your perseverance, your ability to think outside the box and your endless support!

In addition to Nouchine Hadjikhani and Christopher Gillberg, I would also like to thank Jakob Åsberg Johnels, Elena Orekhova and Tatiana Stroganova, who gave me permission to include in the book the case report they have written about my memory difficulties.

And last but surely not least, I also want to thank my family: Despite my memory difficulties, you will naturally always have your extraordinary places in my heart!!

Appendix

Brief descriptions of brain areas I address:

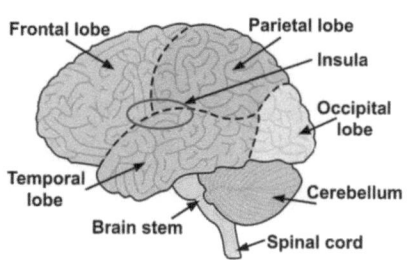

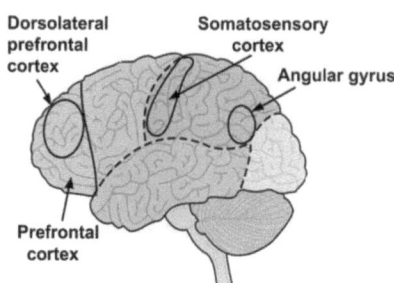

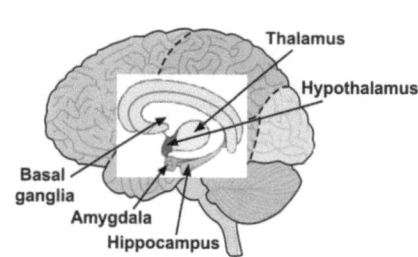

Figure 2: The first image shows, among other things, the different lobes of the brain, although the insula is not visible from the outside because it is located deep down in the lateral fissure. The second image shows the approximate location of some of the cortex areas I mention in the text. And in the dorsolateral prefrontal cortex are thus parts of our working memory located. The image below shows some of the essential structures that lie deep inside the cerebrum, in what is called the limbic system.

Amygdala: A small, almond-shaped structure deep inside our cerebrum (one in each hemisphere). It can be said to be the hub of our emotional network and is thus absolutely necessary for our emotional life, but also for us to be able to create emotional memories. Above all, emotions of the type of fear, horror and anger are associated with this structure. It works closely with the autonomic nervous system.

245

Angular gyrus (AG): area located in the posterior part of our parietal lobes, on the border with the temporal and occipital lobes. Right AG is, for example, essential when it comes to the awareness of our own body and what happens if we, for instance, move in a certain way. It also helps us to distinguish between right and left. Left AG mainly handles more complex semantic functions, which are absolutely necessary for us to read, write and interpret words and texts. But it is also essential when it comes to recalling memories, and then also evaluate whether they are true or perhaps rather illogical. And there are theories that it then not only helps to bring out these memories, but is also responsible for and add the contextual details to our autobiographical memories.

Autonomic nervous system: The part of our nervous system that we don't consciously control. It regulates our most fundamental life processes, such as breathing, heart rate, digestion and metabolism.

Basal ganglia: A collection of nerve cell nuclei deep inside our cerebrum. Their primary function is by sorting information from the cerebral cortex to regulate and ensure that our muscle movements become appropriate and well-coordinated, so that, for example, they don't become too rigid or our muscles cramp. But they are also important in various processes related to consciousness, memory and planning. For example, they are essential for our procedural memory, but also when it comes to our habits and routines.

Brainstem: The part that connects our brain – via the lowest part, the midbrain (where, among others, the thalamus and hypothalamus are found) – with the spinal cord. Here passes neural pathways that transmit signals from the brain to the body, and vice versa. But there are also areas that regulate things that we don't control with the will but are managed autonomously, such as breathing, metabolism, heart activity, etcetera.

Cerebral cortex: The outer, pleated layer that surrounds our cerebrum, which is about three to five millimetres thick. It is divided into two hemispheres, each with four lobes: the frontal lobe, parietal lobe, temporal lobe, and occipital lobe. Insula is sometimes counted as a fifth lob but also as part of the temporal lobe.

Cerebellum: It is located at the back of our skull, below the cerebrum. It is responsible for our coordination and balance, and it is also vital when it comes to planning and implementing movements. Together with the basal ganglia, it is therefore essential for our procedural memory. It also plays an important role in cognition, that had been ignored for a long time, but is increasingly being recognized.

Default Mode Network (DMN): A network consisting of brain structures that are active even when we are not concentrating on a specific task or something outside of ourselves. Like when, for example, we daydream, recalls memories; think about ourselves, our lives and the people around us; or maybe not thinking about anything at all. But even when we do all the daily chores that go on routine. This is our brain's auto mode or starting position, and areas that are part of this network include the medial prefrontal cortex, hippocampus, and angular gyrus – and more that I don't mention here.

EMDR (Eye Movement Desensitization and Reprocessing): A psychotherapy in which so-called bilateral (double-sided) stimulation is used to activate the two hemispheres of the brain alternately. This is believed to facilitate the processing of traumatic memories and create conditions for new thoughts and perspectives to take place. Usually, the stimulation occurs through eye movements, that the patient follows the therapist's finger that is moved from side to side while confronting a painful memory. More information is available, for example, on this page on the internet: http://www.emdria.org/.

Entorhinal cortex: The part of the paralimbic cortex directly adjacent to the hippocampus, which both processes information itself and transmits such to and from that structure. Together with the hippocampus, it is thus a crucial area for our episodic memories – it is, among others, one of the worst affected areas by Alzheimer's disease – but also when it comes to our spatial perception and navigational ability.

Gyrus: These are the ridges and elevations of which our cerebrum's cortex consists. (One gyrus, several gyri).

Hippocampus: A seahorse-shaped (hence the name) structure deep inside our cerebrum (one hippocampus in each hemisphere). Its most important task is to help us create semantic and episodic memories. Still, it is also vital when it comes to our ability to orient ourselves in space or surroundings. Together with the adjacent entorhinal cortex, the area may thus be called our inner GPS.

Hypothalamus: One of the most critical areas of our brain, for here are a large number of nuclei and areas that control what is necessary

248

for our own and human survival. These are, for example, hunger and satiety, thirst, lust and discomfort, sleep and mating behaviour. It is also responsible for maintaining the right balance in our internal body environment, the so-called homeostasis. It thus manages control mechanisms for blood pressure, body temperature, metabolism and secretion of various hormones.

Insula: A vital part of the somatosensory system in the temporal lobe but is often seen as a brain lobe of its own. It is hidden at the bottom of the side fissure that marks the boundary between the frontal lobe, the parietal lobe and the temporal lobe. It receives signals from our internal organs, positive and negative. But it also receives pain impulses from the body and registers disturbances in the autonomic nervous system. This is an essential brain structure when it comes to our emotions and our understanding of them.

Limbic system: After the brainstem and cerebellum, this is the developmentally oldest part of our brain. The area is located deep inside the cerebrum and is sometimes also called the emotional brain. Here we find, among others, the structures amygdala, hippocampus and hypothalamus. The area has the primary responsibility when it comes to emotions, behaviour, memory and sense of smell.

Paralimbic cortex: The cerebral cortex closest to the limbic system, which transmits information from and to higher cortical areas such as the sensory and somatosensory cortex.

Sensory cortex: Areas in our cerebrum that receive and process different sensory impressions. For example, visual impressions are received by the visual cortex in our occipital lobes, while the auditory cortex receives auditory impressions in our temporal lobes.

Somatosensory cortex: This area is located at the front of our parietal lobes, and it receives and processes all information from the body's skin and musculoskeletal system.

Thalamus: The structure might be called the post office or switching station of our brain, since it receives all incoming sensory signals (except olfactory sensations) and then transmits them on to other parts of the brain. It is also an essential part of, for example, the network that controls our will-driven movements, both when it comes to initiating and fine-tuning them.

Some of the words used to describe the location of the brain's various areas:

Dorsal: Upperside.
Lateral: Outside, away from the midline of the brain.
Medial: Inside, towards the midline of the brain.
Ventral: Underside.

These can then be combined as, for example: dorsolateral (located on the outside of the top of the brain), ventrolateral (located on the outside of the bottom of the brain) or ventromedial (located on the bottom of the brain, inside at the midline).

The importance of the body in the creation of autobiographical memories.

That the body is so important to have access to in order to create autobiographical memories has been established in a study conducted at The Karolinska Institute, which was then published in the scientific journal PNAS.

There, 84 students were allowed to study and then undergo four verbal questionings that were made a little extra memorable with an actor's help. Two of the inquiries were experienced from an ordinary perspective from their own body. In contrast, the other two, through a created illusion – with the help of VR glasses – were experienced from a perspective of being outside their body.

A week later, the students had to undergo various memory tests while their brains were imaging using an fMRI camera. It then turned out that they remembered the "out-of-body" questionings much worse than those that had been experienced from an ordinary perspective. And brain imaging revealed a crucial difference in the hippocampus, because when they tried to remember the "out-of-body" questionings, the activity there was wholly eliminated, unlike when they remembered the other inquiries. However, activity was found in the prefrontal cortex, so the students truly made an effort to remember.

The researchers' interpretation of the study is that there is a close connection between body experience and memory. Our brain simply needs to be informed that we are actually in our body in order to create uniform long-term memories; otherwise, the memory process is disrupted, and the memory becomes fragmentary instead.

A case report of severely impaired autobiographical memory in a woman with Asperger syndrome

Nouchine Hadjikhani [1,2,*], Jakob Åsberg Johnels [2], Elena Orekhova[2,3,4], Tatiana Stroganova [3,4], Christopher Gillberg [2], Malin Bohman.

1. MGH/MIT/HST Martinos Center for Biomedical Imaging, Harvard Medical School, Charlestown, Massachusetts, USA.
2. Gillberg Neuropsychiatry Centre (GNC), University of Gothenburg, Gothenburg, Sweden.
3. Moscow State University of Psychology and Education, Center for Neurocognitive Research (MEG Center), Moscow, Russia.
4. Autism Research Laboratory, Moscow State University of Psychology and Education, Moscow, Russia.

Correspondence to:
Nouchine Hadjikhani, MD, PhD
nouchine.hadjikhani@gnc.gu.se

Abstract

Here, we report the case of MB, a 53 year-old woman, who came to our neurodevelopmental/neuropsychiatric clinic due to suspicion of Asperger syndrome. Her behavioral/clinical profile was consistent with this diagnosis. In addition, a severely impaired autobiographical memory was confirmed in the face of otherwise normal neuropsychological functioning, including general IQ, working memory, episodic (long-term) memory and visual memory. MRI data indicated reduced bilateral hippocampal volume compared to age-matched female controls, with an imbalance in volume between the left and the right hippocampus, favoring the left. These findings are consistent with a few previous reports of severely impaired autobiographical memory. In addition, MEG/EEG data revealed abnormal activity in certain brain regions, including the left temporal region and in the angular gyrus, areas known to be associated with autobiographic memory formation.

Introduction

"I am walking through life with an eraser on my back"

Autobiographical memory allows us to build our own identity, remembering our past and projecting images of ourselves into the future. In this paper, we report the case of MB (one of the co-authors of this paper), a 53-year-old woman, who came to our neurodevelopmental/neuropsychiatric clinic due to suspicion of Asperger syndrome, which was confirmed by one of the co-authors (CG, who is one of the most experienced clinicians in the field in the world). Extremely reduced eye contact, strict/rigid routines, very few friendships, bouts of anxiety, attention to details, strong focus on certain themes, and a history of eating disorders that were present in MB are all common features in the presentation of Asperger syndrome in females (Attwood, 2007; Gillberg & Gillberg, 1989; Goin-Kochel, Mackintosh, & Myers, 2006; Knickmeyer, Wheelwright, & Baron-Cohen, 2008; Kopp & Gillberg, 1992; Lai et al., 2011; Mattila et al., 2007; Wentz et al., 2005). In addition, severely impaired autobiographical memory (AM) was noted at first assessment. Previous medical and psychiatric evaluations suggested that her problems were by no means simple, with a complex history of childhood trauma, and a chronic pain condition. On the other hand, MB is an unusually intellectually curious individual with an impressive knowledge about neuroscience in general and her own condition in particular.

255

In this case report, we focus on the nature of MB's AM deficit, with the aim of contributing to a small but growing literature on Severely Deficient Autobiographical Memory (SDAM) (Palombo, Alain, Söderlund, Khuu, & Levine, 2015), for review, see (Palombo, Sheldon, & Levine, 2018), a term for a condition that MB herself relates to. We report neuropsychological data in order to support the selectivity of AM impairment in the cognitive profile of the patient. Using anatomical MRI, MEG and EEG recordings, we provide a thorough clinical characterization of brain structure and function. In particular, we want to confirm and extend previous findings by examining hippocampal volume (Palombo, Bacopulos, et al., 2018) a key area for the formation of memories, including AM.

We discuss how the neurophysiological findings might explain the presence of SDAM in this case and also in the light of other, similar, published case reports. Finally, we consider the potential connection between Asperger syndrome and SDAM.

Case findings

Informed consent to publish this clinical case report is available in MB's medical charts. In addition, MEG data have been collected under a study approved by the Gothenburg Regional Ethical Review Board.

Neuropsychological and symptomatic profile:

We used a battery of tests and self-report questionnaires to assess different aspects of the difficulties encountered by MB in order to identify strengths and challenges, with a specific aim of characterizing the selectivity – or otherwise – of the AM deficits. Critically, virtually all the neuropsychological test results were normal or above normal. This includes her general full-scale IQ (which gathered from her medical charts), verbal short-term memory and long-term memory, narrative comprehension and memory. Perhaps especially noteworthy in the context of AM deficits, is her strong performance on the Discourse comprehension test (Welland, Lubinski, & Higginbotham, 2002) which assesses episodic memory for narratives. Still, given the fact that MB reported strong interest in literary fiction reading, it seems reasonable that episodic memory per se would not be an area of difficulty.

The assessments made were motivated by previous research on AM deficits. In particular, the three participants in the Palombo study (2015) tended to score poorly on the REY complex figure test, indicative of visual mental imagery deficits. However, this was not obviously the case for MB.

There are no "gold standard" tests of autobiographic memory. We used the modified Crovitz interview (Philippi, Rousseau, et al., 2015) to measure the ability to recreate autobiographical memories about specific episodes of the patient's life. This is done by eliciting memories with cue words and asking the patient to describe and date that specific memory as well as they can. MB was found to perform very poorly, considerably below the suggested clinical cut off (Ernst et al., 2013). The assessor noted during the 2 hour long interview that emotionally charged memories – including traumas and very joyful experiences – tend to be better remembered, even though still lacking an autobiographic quality, whereas more everyday experiences seem to quickly fade.

The Toronto Alexithymia Scale (TAS) and Autism Quotient (AQ) scores cover self-reported alexithymia and autistic traits, respectively. The results revealed marked features relating to these symptomatic features. The TAS consists of three subscales assessing Difficulty Describing Feelings, Difficulty Identifying Feelings, and Externally-Oriented Thinking. While MB showed extremely externally-oriented thinking, she reported high symptoms on the description and the identification of feelings, resulting in a score that was just below clinical cut-off. The score on the AQ test indicated the presence of autism. Asperger type of autism was confirmed clinically by two medical doctors (CG and NH) with considerable diagnostic experience of autism and related disorders.

MB's sensory profile tested by Adolescent/Adult Sensory Profile (A/ASP) questionnaire (Brown and Dunn, 2002) was also consistent with that observed in Asperger studies, with significantly lower scores in sensory seeking, and higher scores in sensory sensitivity and sensory avoidance.

Test name	Cognitive construct	Score	Interpretation based on norms or clinically suggested cut offs
Modified Crovitz test	Autobiographical memory	35%	Impaired: cut off 74
WASI FSIQ	General intelligence	118	Normal or above normal according to norms (mean 100)
Verbal IQ	Linguistic reasoning ability	113	Normal according to norms
Nonverbal (performance)	Nonverbal reasoning ability	116	Normal or above according to norms
Rey AVL	Visual mental imagery while copying and long term recall of visual-spatial information	T-scores of 51/49/41 for immediate recall, delayed recall and recognition, respectively	Normal according to norms
Discourse comprehension test	Narrative comprehension and memory for literal and inferential story details	97% correct	Normal or above normal: mean score of 92.5 in normal adult participants
Spatial span	Visual short term memory	Stanine 5-7	Normal according to norms
Digit span	Verbal short term memory	Stanine 4	Normal according to norms
TAS	Alexithymia – difficulties	Raw score 60	Bordeline impaired. Cut-off > 61.
AQ	Autistic personality traits	35	Above normal (clinical cut-off = 32)
A/ASP	Low registration	31	Normal (24-35)
A/ASP	Sensation seeking	34	Very low (43-56)
A/ASP	Sensory sensitivity	55	Very high (26-41)
A/ASP	Sensation avoiding	49	High (27-41)

Table 1: *Neuropsychological tests.*

Neuroanatomical data:

Informed by the study reporting decreased hippocampal volume and hippocampal asymmetry in SDAM (Palombo et al., 2015), we acquired high-resolution 3D T1 MP-RAGE MRI scan (voxel size 1x1x1mm, acquisition matrix 256x256, TR=4.48) when MB was 50 years old. FreeSurfer segmentation was used to measure the volume of the hippocampus. This was compared with the volume of a control group consisting of 19 healthy females, aged 50.74± 5.56 (p=0.57, ns).

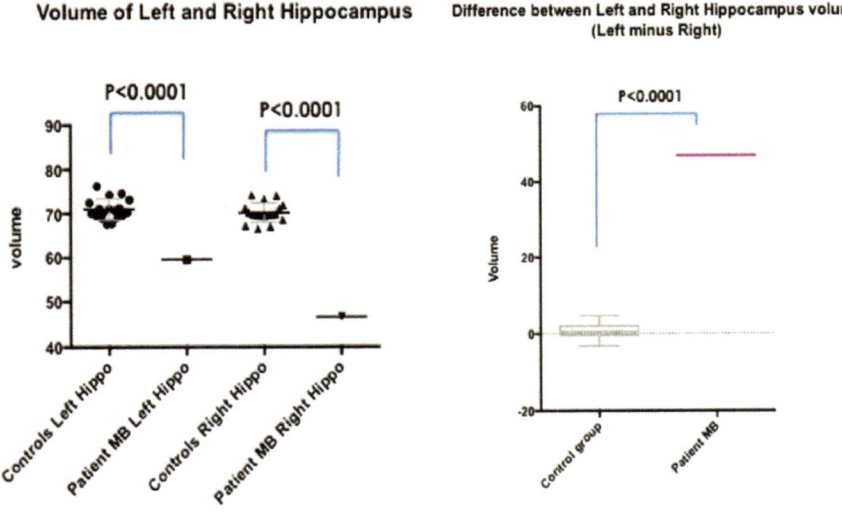

Figure 1: Hippocampal Volume. The left panel illustrates the difference between MB and controls for the left and the right hippocampal volume. The right panel shows the difference between the left and the right hippocampal volume in the control group (null) and in MB, who has a difference favoring the left hippocampus.

Our data indicated that both left and the right hippocampus in MB were significantly smaller than in the controls (p<0.0001), which is partly similar to (Palombo et al., 2015), who only found a decreased volume in the right hippocampus. In addition, and similarly to the findings reported in (Palombo et al., 2015), in MB the right hippocampus was significantly smaller than the left (p<0.0001), whereas in the control group right and left hippocampus had the same volume (**Figure** 1). Notably, the volume of MB's amygdalae was not significantly different from the controls.

MEG/EEG data:

MEG data were recorded with whole-head magnetoencephalographic (MEG) device with 204 planar gradiometers and 102 magnetometers (Triux Elekta Neuromag) and sampled at 1000 Hz. Four head coils were used for continuous head position monitoring. Additional 4 bipolar EEG electrodes were placed for ECG and EOG measurements, and 2 more electrodes were positioned to the chest to record the heart rate. Data were collected during rest and during the presence of a visual task meant to provoke gamma oscillations (for a detailed description see, (Orekhova et al., 2018). Despite the fact that MB never had any reported seizure, there were three types of abnormal electrographic patterns in MB's results:

First, strictly left-lateralized abundant continuous monomorphic/rhythmic alpha activity, regular in shape with prolonged duration (up to 30 sec) and predominant frequency of 10 Hz were observed over the left temporal lobe (**Figure 2**). This activity was intermixed with the infrequent and short (<1 s) rhythmic trains of theta oscillations (7-8 Hz) with unilateral left temporal scalp topography (**Figure 2**). Unilateral temporal alpha-theta activity was clearly non-reactive to the presence/absence of the visual task. Its cortical sources were confined to basal/medial (theta) and lateral (alpha) surface of left temporal lobe (**Figure 2**).

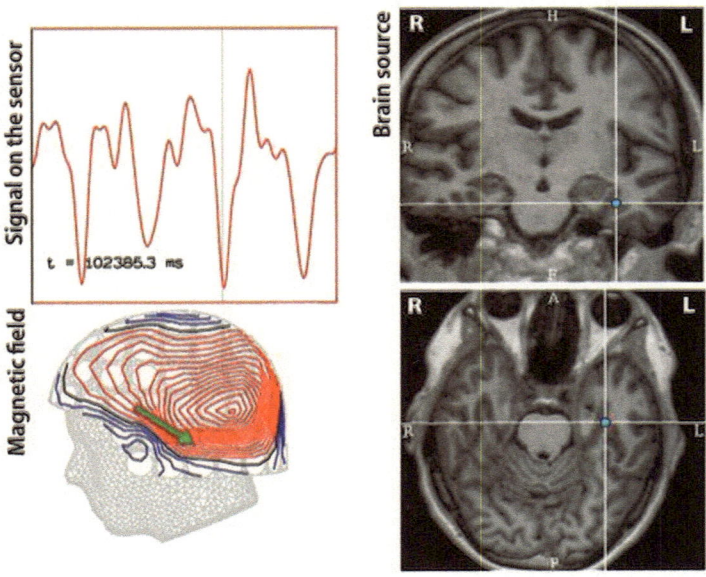

Figure 2: Abnormal activity in left temporal lobe.

Second, single epileptiform spikes and sharp waves were observed over the left temporal lobe. Their sources were predominantly localized to the posterior part of left superior temporal sulcus/middle temporal gyrus and the adjacent regions of angular gyrus (**Figure 3** – purple oval). The second scattered cluster of sources occupied the basal surface of left temporal lobe (**Figure 3** - yellow oval).

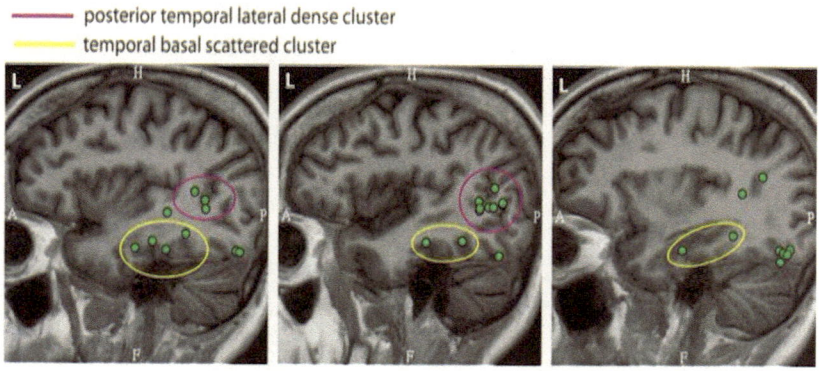

Figure 3: *Location of clusters of abnormal electrical activity in left hemisphere.*

Third, frequent occipital spikes and spike-and-wave complexes. Occipital epileptiform transients occurred more frequently (2 events per 10 s) during prolonged visual stimulation than during passive wakefulness. Their sources formed three dense cortical clusters: the first one at the cuneus region of left occipital lobe; the second and third symmetric clusters occupied the basal surface of occipital lobes in the occipitotemporal sulcus/fusiform gyrus.

Discussion

In the present case report, we found anatomical (hippocampal volume) and electrophysiological (epileptiform transients in the left temporal and angular gyrus, as well as in the occipital cortex bilaterally) evidence of abnormalities that could be directly linked to the presence of SDAM, although a causative link cannot be established.

A few recent case studies have shown the presence of SDAM in healthy individuals (for review, see Palombo, Sheldon, et al., 2018). In the case series described by Palombo and colleagues, SDAM individuals did not show impairments in neuropsychological tests assessing attention, perception, working memory and executive functions, and no impairment either in learning and retaining factual information. However, visual imagery was described as abnormal in these individuals, who otherwise functioned normally in daily life. In terms of brain imaging findings, SDAM individuals had right-lateralized reduction of hippocampal volume (Palombo, Bacopulos, et al., 2018), and functional MRI revealed reduced task-based activation during autobiographical recollection in the medial prefrontal cortex and the precuneus (Sheldon, Farb, Palombo, & Levine, 2016). Of note, impaired emotional autobiographical memory has been associated with right amygdala–hippocampal atrophy (Philippi, Botzung, et al., 2015). Electrophysiological data have been reported in two previous studies on SDAM, one indicating abnormal ERP for a recollection task (Palombo et al., 2015), and another one displaying reduced gamma and theta phase coupling during autobiographical recollection (Fuentemilla, Palombo, & Levine, 2018).

The role of the angular gyrus in autobiographical memory has recently been recognized, and a recent study reported selective reduction of free recall following continuous theta burst stimulation (cTBS) (Bonnici, Cheke, Green, FitzGerald, & Simons, 2018). Interestingly, this was also accompanied by a reduction of first-person experience autobiographical episodes. As underlined by (Ramanan, Piguet, & Irish, 2018), the role of the left angular gyrus in memory has been debated a lot, and these authors put forward a model that they coined as the Contextual Integration Model in which the core elements of an event (e.g. people, event, time, location) are coded in the medial temporal lobe, while multimodal contextual details become integrated and represented in the angular gyrus. In the case of MB, abnormalities in the function of both medial temporal lobe and angular gyrus, as evidenced by epileptiform transients, may underlie the severity of her memory deficits.

In the history of neuropsychology and behavioral neurology, Asperger syndrome has been linked with superior memory performance. Indeed, Luria reported, in the Mind of a Mnemonist (Luria, 1968), the combination of a highly superior memory with characteristics of what is nowadays often diagnosed as Asperger syndrome (literal understanding of language, adherence to strict routines, etc). Research on individuals with exceptional memories have reported that this was sometimes associated with savant conditions associated with Asperger syndrome (e.g. (Bor, Billington, & Baron-Cohen, 2007)) however, recent studies have also shown that autobiographical memory may be compromised in Asperger syndrome (Crane, Pring, Jukes, & Goddard, 2012; Tanweer, Rathbone, & Souchay, 2010).

Conclusion

There have been only a few case-reports of SDAM in the literature, and most of them were reported in otherwise healthy individuals, albeit very little detail regarding any behavioral/psychiatric problem has been reported. Our case-report indicates a possible association of SDAM, reduced hippocampal volume, and epileptiform transients in areas of the brain that are crucial for autobiographical memory, together with Asperger type autism, in a patient with a complex psychiatric history and an unusually impressive capacity to self-reflect about the implications of her condition. Her vivid and detailed description of her condition gives us a rich first-person perspective into something that is otherwise rather difficult to grasp for a typical individual, which is: what is it like to go through life without remembering your own past.

References:

• Attwood, T. (2007). *The complete guide to Asperger's syndrome.* Philadelphia, PA: Jessica Kingley Publishers.

• Bonnici, H. M., Cheke, L. G., Green, D. A. E., FitzGerald, T. H. B., & Simons, J. S. (2018). Specifying a causal role for angular gyrus in autobiographical memory. *J Neurosci.* doi:10.1523/JNEUROSCI.1239-18.2018

• Bor, D., Billington, J., & Baron-Cohen, S. (2007). Savant memory for digits in a case of synaesthesia and Asperger syndrome is related to hyperactivity in the lateral prefrontal cortex. *Neurocase, 13*(5), 311-319. doi:10.1080/13554790701844945

• Brown, C. E., & Dunn, W. (2002). *Adolescent-Adult Sensory Profile: user's manual.* San Antonio, Tex: Pearson

• Crane, L., Pring, L., Jukes, K., & Goddard, L. (2012). Patterns of autobiographical memory in adults with autism spectrum disorder. *J Autism Dev Disord, 42*(10), 2100-2112. doi:10.1007/s10803-012-1459-2

• Ernst, A., Blanc, F., Voltzenlogel, V., de Seze, J., Chauvin, B., & Manning, L. (2013). Autobiographical memory in multiple sclerosis patients: assessment and cognitive facilitation. *Neuropsychol Rehabil, 23*(2), 161-181. doi:10.1080/09602011.2012.724355

• Fuentemilla, L., Palombo, D. J., & Levine, B. (2018). Gamma phase-synchrony in autobiographical memory: Evidence from magneto-encephalography and severely deficient autobiographical memory.

Neuropsychologia, 110, 7–13. doi:10.1016/j.neuropsychologia.2017.08.020

• Gillberg, I. C., & Gillberg, C. (1989). Asperger syndrome – some epidemiological considerations: a research note. *J Child Psychol Psychiatry, 30*(4), 631–638.

• Goin-Kochel, R. P., Mackintosh, V. H., & Myers, B. J. (2006). How many doctors does it take to make an autism spectrum diagnosis? *Autism, 10*(5), 439–451. doi:10.1177/1362361306066601

• Knickmeyer, R. C., Wheelwright, S., & Baron-Cohen, S. B. (2008). Sex-typical play: masculinization/defeminization in girls with an autism spectrum condition. *J Autism Dev Disord, 38*(6), 1028–1035. doi:10.1007/s10803-007-0475-0

• Kopp, S., & Gillberg, C. (1992). Girls with social deficits and learning problems: autism, atypical Asperger syndrome or a variant of these conditions. *European Child and Adolescent Psychiatry, 1*(2), 89–99.

• Lai, M. C., Lombardo, M. V., Pasco, G., Ruigrok, A. N., Wheelwright, S. J., Sadek, S. A., Baron-Cohen, S. (2011). A behavioral comparison of male and female adults with high functioning autism spectrum conditions. *Plos One, 6*(6), e20835. doi:10.1371/journal.pone.0020835

• Luria, A. R. (1968). *The Mind of a Mnemonist: A Little Book About a Vast Memory.* NY: New York Basic Books.

• Mattila, M. L., Kielinen, M., Jussila, K., Linna, S. L., Bloigu, R., Ebeling, H., & Moilanen, I. (2007). An epidemiological and diagnostic study of Asperger syndrome according to four sets of diagnostic criteria. *J Am Acad Child Adolesc Psychiatry*, *46*(5), 636-646. doi:10.1097/chi.0b013e318033ff42

• Orekhova, E. V., Sysoeva, O. V., Schneiderman, J. F., Lundström, S., Galuta, I. A., Goiaeva, D. E., Stroganova, T. A. (2018). Input-dependent modulation of MEG gamma oscillations reflects gain control in the visual cortex. *Sci Rep*, *8*(1), 8451. doi:10.1038/s41598-018-26779-6

• Palombo, D. J., Alain, C., Söderlund, H., Khuu, W., & Levine, B. (2015). Severely deficient autobiographical memory (SDAM) in healthy adults: A new mnemonic syndrome. *Neuropsychologia*, *72*, 105-118. doi:10.1016/j.neuropsychologia.2015.04.012

• Palombo, D. J., Bacopulos, A., Amaral, R. S. C., Olsen, R. K., Todd, R. M., Anderson, A. K., & Levine, B. (2018). Episodic autobiographical memory is associated with variation in the size of hippocampal subregions. *Hippocampus*, *28*(2), 69-75. doi:10.1002/hipo.22818

• Palombo, D. J., Sheldon, S., & Levine, B. (2018). Individual Differences in Autobiographical Memory. Trends *Cogn Sci*, *22*(7), 583-597. doi:10.1016/j.tics.2018.04.007

• Philippi, N., Botzung, A., Noblet, V., Rousseau, F., Despres, O., Cretin, B., Manning, L. (2015). Impaired emotional autobiographical memory associated with right amygdalar-hippocampal atrophy in Alzheimer's disease patients. *Front Aging Neurosci*, *7*, 21. doi:10.3389/fnagi.2015.00021

• Philippi, N., Rousseau, F., Noblet, V., Botzung, A., Despres, O., Cretin, B., Manning, L. (2015). Different Temporal Patterns of Specific and General Autobiographical Memories across the Lifespan in Alzheimer's Disease. *Behav Neurol, 2015*, 963460. doi:10.1155/2015/963460

• Ramanan, S., Piguet, O., & Irish, M. (2018). Rethinking the Role of the Angular Gyrus in Remembering the Past and Imagining the Future: The Contextual Integration Model. *Neuroscientist, 24*(4), 342-352. doi:10.1177/1073858417735514

• Sheldon, S., Farb, N., Palombo, D. J., & Levine, B. (2016). Intrinsic medial temporal lobe connectivity relates to individual differences in episodic autobiographical remembering. *Cortex, 74*, 206-216. doi:10.1016/j.cortex.2015.11.005

• Tanweer, T., Rathbone, C. J., & Souchay, C. (2010). Autobiographical memory, autonoetic consciousness, and identity in Asperger syndrome. *Neuropsychologia, 48*(4), 900-908. doi:10.1016/j.neuropsychologia.2009.11.007

• Welland, R. J., Lubinski, R., & Higginbotham, D. J. (2002). Discourse comprehension test performance of elders with dementia of the Alzheimer type. *J Speech Lang Hear Res, 45*(6), 1175-1187.

• Wentz, E., Lacey, J. H., Waller, G., Råstam, M., Turk, J., & Gillberg, C. (2005). Childhood onset neuropsychiatric disorders in adult eating disorder patients. A pilot study. *Eur Child Adolesc Psychiatry, 14*(8), 431-437. doi:10.1007/s00787-005-0494-3

Selected literature

I have read a great deal about the memory over the years and therefore don't remember all the books I have obtained knowledge from and maybe should refer to. However, the books and studies I, for instance, took help from when I wrote this text were these.

Articles and non-fiction:

• Bergouignan, L., Nyberg, L., & Ehrsson, H. (2014). Out-of-body-induced hippocampal amnesia. *PNAS*, 111(12), pp. 4421-4426. DOI: 10.1073/pnas.1318801111

• Bonnici, H. M., Chadwick, M. J., Lutti, A., Hassabis, D., Weiskopf, N., & Maguire, E. A. (2012). Detecting representations of recent and remote autobiographical memories in vmPFC and hippocampus. *The Journal of Neuroscience*, 32(47), pp. 16982-16991. DOI: 10.1523/JNEUROSCI.2475-12.2012

• Bonnici, H., Cheke, L., Green, D., FitzGerald, T., & Simons, J. (2018). Specifying a causal role for angular gyrus in autobiographical memory. Preprint. *BioRxiv*, 323733. DOI: 10.1101/323733

• Cohen, Gillian. (1996). *Memory in the real world*. Hove: Psychology Press.

• Corkin, Suzanne. (2014). *Permanent Present Tense*. London: Penguine Books.

• Craig, Michael & Dewar, Michaela. (2018). Rest-related consolidation protects the fine detail of new memories. *Scientific Reports*, vol. 8, article number: 6857. DOI: 10.1038/s41598-018-25313-y

• Damasio, Antonio R. (1994). *Descartes' Error: Emotion, Reason, and the Human Brain.* New York: Putnam Publishing.

• Damasio, Antonio R. (2003). *Looking for Spinoza: Joy, Sorrow and the Feeling Brain.* San Diego: Harcourt.

• Dance, C.J., Jaquiery, M., Eagleman, D.M., Porteous, D., Zeman, A., Simner, J. (2021). What is the relationship between Aphantasia, Synaesthesia and Autism? *Consciousness and Cognition,* vol. 89, 103087. DOI: 10.1016/j.concog.2021.103087

• Dawes, A.J., Keogh, R., Andrillon, T. et al. (2020). A cognitive profile of multi-sensory imagery, memory and dreaming in aphantasia. *Scientific Reports,* vol. 10, 10022. DOI: 10.1038/s41598-020-65705-7

• Euston, D. R., Gruber, A. J. & McNaughton, B. L. (2012). The Role of Medial Prefrontal Cortex in Memory and Decision Making. *Neuron*, 76(6), pp. 1057-1070. DOI: 10.1016/j.neuron.2012.12.002

• Goleman, Daniel. (1995). *Emotional Intelligence.* New York: Bantam Books.

• Jonker, T. R., Dimsdale-Zucker, H., Ritchey, M., Clarke, A. & Ranganath, C. (2018). Neural reactivation in parietal cortex enhances memory for episodically linked information. *PNAS*, 115(43), pp. 11084-11089. DOI: 10.1073/pnas.1800006115

• LeDoux, Joseph. (1999). *The Emotional Brain*. London: Phoenix.

• McCormick, C., Rosenthal, C. R., Miller, T. D. & Maguire, E. A. (2018). Mind-Wandering in People with Hippocampal Damage. *The Journal of Neuroscience*, 38(11), pp. 2745-2754. DOI: 10.1523/JNEUROSCI.1812-17.2018

• Padmanabhan, A., Lynch, C. J., Schaer, M. & Menon, V. (2017). The Default Mode Network in Autism. *Biological Psychiatry: Cognitive Neuroscience and Neuroimaging*, 2(6), pp. 476-486. DOI: 10.1016/j.bpsc.2017.04.004

• Palombo, D. J., Alain, C., Söderlund, H., Khuu, W. & Levine, B. (2015). Severely deficient autobiographical memory (SDAM) in healthy adults: A new mnemonic syndrome. *Neuropsychologia*, 72, pp.105–118. DOI: 10.1016/j.neuropsychologia.2015.04.012

• Phelps, Elisabeth A. (2004). Human emotion and memory: interactions of the amygdala and hippocampal complex. *Current Opinion in Neurobiology*, 14(2), pp. 198-202. DOI: 10.1016/j.conb.2004.03.015

• Ramanan, S., Piguet, O. & Irish, M. (2018). Rethinking the Role of the Angular Gyrus in Remembering the Past and Imagining the Future: The Contextual Integration Model. *The Neuroscientist,* 24(4), pp. 342-352. DOI: 10.1177/1073858417735514

• Söderlund, H., Moscovitch, M., Kumar, N., Mandic, M. & Levine, B. (2011). As time goes by: hippocampal connectivity changes with remoteness of autobiographical memory retrieval. *Hippocampus*, 22(4), pp. 670-679. DOI: 10.1002/hipo.20927

• Tsao, A., Sugar, J., Lu, L., Wang, C., Knierim, J. J., Moser, M.-B., & Moser, E. I. (2018). Integrating time from experience in the lateral entorhinal cortex. *Nature*, vol. 561, pp. 57-62. DOI: 10.1038/s41586-018-0459-6

• Tulving, Endel. (2000). Episodic memory and autonoetic awareness. In Endel Tulving & Fergus I. M. Craik (red.). *The Oxford handbook of memory*. New York: Oxford University Press.

• Walker, Matthew. (2017). *Why We Sleep: The New Science of Sleep and Dreams*. New York: Penguin Random House.

• Wasling, Pontus. (2013). *Minnet, fram och tillbaka*. Stockholm: Volante.

• Yerys, B. E., Gordon, E. M., Abrams, D. N., Satterthwaite, T. D., Weinblatt, R., Jankowski, K. F., Strang, J., Kenworthy, L., Gaillard, W. D. & Vaidya, C. J. (2015). Default mode network segregation and social deficits in autism spectrum disorder: Evidence from non-medicated children. *NeuroImage: Clinical*, vol. 9, pp. 223-232. DOI: 10.1016/j.nicl.2015.07.018

• Zeman, A., Milton, F., Della Sala, S., Dewar, M., Frayling, T., Gaddum, J., Hattersley, A., Heuerman-Williamson, B., Jones, K., MacKisack, M., Winlove, C. (2020). Phantasia-The psychological significance of lifelong visual imagery vividness extremes. *Cortex*, Sep;130:426-440. DOI: 10.1016/j.cortex.2020.04.003

The quotes are taken from these books:

• Bahlenberg, Majken. (2006). *Flickan i blå stolen.*
Stockholm: Litteratursällskapet.

• Faulkner, William. (1951). *Requiem for a Nun.*
New York: Random House.

• Gerland, Gunilla. (2003). *A Real Person: Life on the Outside.*
London: Souvenir Press Ltd.

• Jinder, Åsa. (1991). *Bli min mamma igen.*
Stockholm: Bonniers.

• Johansson, Iris. (2013). *Ett annorlunda liv.*
Stockholm: Forum.

• Krauss, Nicole. (2002). *Man Walkes Into a Room.*
New York: Doubleday.

• Rynell, Elisabeth. (1990). *En berättelse om Loka.*
Stockholm: Bonniers.

• Voors, Barbara. (2010). *Fantomsmärtor.*
Stockholm: Bonniers.